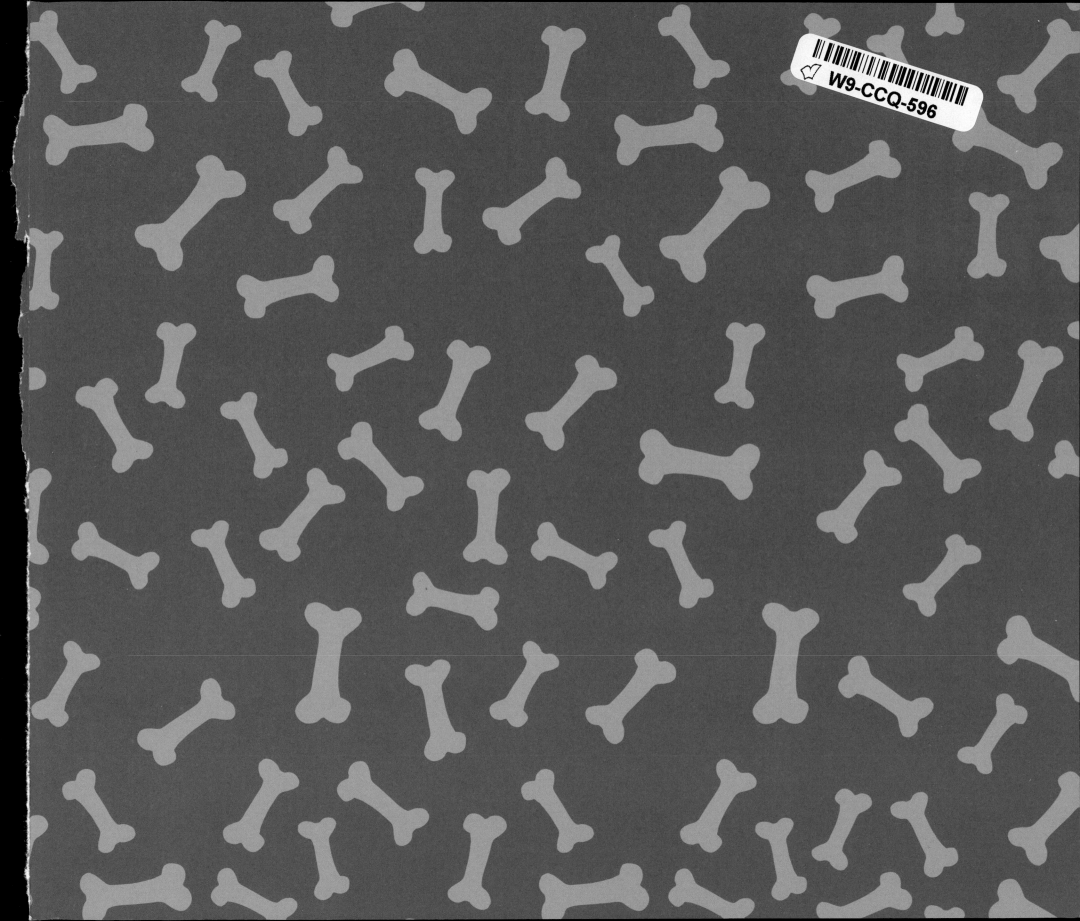

DOGS

A CELEBRATION OF OUR CANINE COMPANIONS

pil

Publications International, Ltd.

TABLE OF CONTENTS

WHAT MAKES DOGS SO SPECIAL?

While the specifics about when, how, and where humans first domesticated dogs are murky, it is a fact that humans and canines have been by each other's side for thousands of years.

Tens of thousands of years ago, humans began to live together with the grey wolf. In time, the wolves became smaller and friendlier and grew closer to their human counterparts. The first dogs emerged.

Historically, different dogs have served different purposes. Shepherd dogs herded farm animals, mastiffs guarded property, and hounds hunted large and small game. Eventually, new breeds served strictly as companions rather than farm or hunting hands (or paws).

Today, about 500 million domestic dogs roam nearly every corner of our world. They comfort the sick, entertain the young, and perform a variety of different tasks. They come in different sizes, shapes, and colors. They have different coats, temperaments, and purposes. Most importantly, dogs provide years of memories, goodwill, and affection.

Dogs highlights 70 of today's most popular breeds. The following pages feature vibrant photos, fun facts, and historical tidbits about some of the world's famous canines.

What makes dogs so special? Turn the page and find out!

AMERICAN WATER SPANIEL

HISTORY

A familiar face around the Great Lakes states (though perhaps less so around other parts of the United States), the American Water Spaniel is a skilled swimmer, retriever, and hunter. This midsize dog boosts plenty of energy and fervor for the outdoors.

A watchdog and family dog, this breed was first introduced to Wisconsin in the mid-1800s. European immigrants tackled the difficulties of hunting waterfowl by breeding what experts suspect were the Irish Water Spaniel, Curly-Coated Retriever, Field Spaniel, and the now-extinct Old English Water Spaniel.

This is a breed that requires daily exercise, be it a game of fetch, a long walk, or other backyard or park games. They'll need it, too, as an American Water Spaniel with too much energy may take up chewing or barking.

CHARACTERISTICS

HEIGHT:
15-18 inches

WEIGHT:
30-45 pounds (male)
25-40 pounds (female)

LIFE EXPECTANCY:
10-14 years

GROUP:
Sporting Group

DID YOU KNOW?

- Wisconsin named the American Water Spaniel its state dog in 1985.

- F. J. Pfeifer of New London, Wisconsin, is credited with saving the breed from extinction in the early 1900s. One of his own dogs named "Curly Pfeifer" was the first registered American Water Spaniel.

- Only about 3,000 American Water Spaniels exist today, according to the American Water Spaniel Club.

- Today, the majority of the breed's owners and breeders are found in Wisconsin, Michigan, and Minnesota.

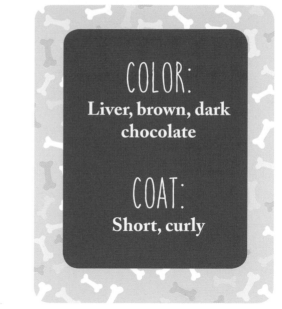

COLOR:
Liver, brown, dark chocolate

COAT:
Short, curly

BRITTANY

HISTORY

A bird hunting and all around versatile dog, the Brittany earns its name from the French province of its origin.

French hunters developed the breed to help hunt a variety of feathery animals. This breeding resulted in a midsize dog that's athletic, handsome, intelligent, and highly energetic (and one with a superb nose). In 1931, the Brittany was introduced to America. After suffering a decline following World War II, the breed rebounded in popularity during the second half of the 20th century.

Besides being an excellent hunting companion, the Brittany is also a personable, friendly dog that, with exposure, jives well with other dogs or animals. The breed is popular among families, but because of the Brittany's active personality, supervision is recommended around small children.

CHARACTERISTICS

HEIGHT:
17.5-20.5 inches

WEIGHT:
30-40 pounds

LIFE EXPECTANCY:
12-14 years

GROUP:
Sporting Group

DID YOU KNOW?

- Paintings and tapestries of the 17th century provide the first visual records of Brittany-like dogs.

- The American Kennel Club Board of Directors approved the deletion of the word "spaniel" in Brittany's name in 1982.

- In France, however, the breed is still known as the Brittany Spaniel.

- The breed consistently earns the American Kennel Club's Dual Champion title for field and herding competitions.

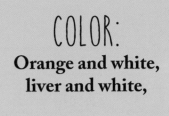

COLOR:
Orange and white, liver and white,

COAT:
Dense, flat, wavy

CHESAPEAKE BAY RETRIEVER

HISTORY

A powerful, well-built duck dog with an oily coat, the Chesapeake Bay Retriever (or Chessie) is a protective, polite dog that makes for an excellent companion. But if an owner simply wants a canine companion, this dog is most certainly not the best pick.

This all-American breed is believed to descend from a pair of Newfoundland dogs aboard a shipwrecked vessel in 1807. Experts believe the dogs Sailor, a red male, and Canton, a black female, mated, and their offspring ultimately spread throughout the region.

The Chessie is a hunting dog through and through. This sporting breed is built to withstand cold waters like Chesapeake Bay, as its thick coat insulates and repels moisture. The Chessie's broad chest and webbed feet help it swim in frigid, challenging waters. Experts do not recommend Chessies for first-time dog owners, for this breed requires proper training, socialization, and lots of exercise.

CHARACTERISTICS

HEIGHT:
23-26 inches (male);
21-24 inches (female)

WEIGHT:
65-80 pounds (male);
55-70 pounds (female)

LIFE EXPECTANCY:
10-13 years

GROUP:
Sporting Group

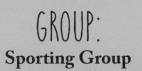

DID YOU KNOW?

- Because of its powerful nose, the Chessie is a valuable bomb and drug detection and search and rescue dog.

- The American Kennel Club registered its first Chessie in 1878.

- Urban legend says a Chessie can retrieve 300 ducks in a day.

- The Chessie can compete in all areas of American Kennel Club competition.

COLOR:
Brown, sedge, deadgrass

COAT:
Thick, dense and wooly undercoat

COCKER SPANIEL

HISTORY

A descendant of the spaniel family, the Cocker Spaniel is one of the most recognizable breeds in the United States. It is one of a handful of spaniels that evolved in Europe over centuries.

Spaniels were ultimately divided into two groups: toys and larger hunting dogs. The larger breeds evolved into land and water spaniels. Named after its excellence in hunting woodcocks, the Cocker excels in field trials, agility, and other performance activities.

Cockers are family dogs that require companionship and a comfortable home. Early socialization is essential, for a poorly trained Cocker may become needlessly shy and fearful of people.

CHARACTERISTICS

HEIGHT:
14.5-15.5 inches (male)

13.5-14.5 (female)

WEIGHT:
25-30 pounds (male)

20-25 pounds (female)

LIFE EXPECTANCY:
10-14 years

GROUP:
Sporting Group

DID YOU KNOW?

- The Cocker is the smallest member of the Sporting Group.

- Disney's 1955 classic movie *Lady and the Tramp* popularized the breed.

- One renowned Cocker Spaniel named My Own Brucie was so popular that, following his death in 1943, the *New York Times* published an obituary for the famed canine.

- Before he became president, Richard Nixon owned a Cocker Spaniel named Checkers.

COLOR:
Variety of colors

COAT:
Medium, curly

ENGLISH SETTER

HISTORY

Trained as an English bird dog more than 400 years ago, the English Setter is a dog equally skilled in tracking and play. Breeders crossed spaniel and pointer breeds to create a new breed that would "set," or quietly sit, when faced with game. This country house dog has a feathery tail, a speckled coat, and an oval-shaped head.

Edward Laverack developed the pure breed in the 1820s, and R. Purcell Llewellin used some of Laverack's dogs to create a new strain for field work at the end of the century. Both types found their way to the United States by the early 1900s.

The English Setter makes for a fine family dog thanks to its calm personality. This breed requires plenty of exercise and open spaces. And if you own a yard, make sure you have a sturdy fence: English Setters are known for their jumping and digging abilities.

CHARACTERISTICS

HEIGHT:
**25-27 inches (male);
23-25 inches (female)**

WEIGHT:
**65-80 pounds (male);
45-55 pounds (female)**

LIFE EXPECTANCY:
12 years

GROUP:
Sporting Group

DID YOU KNOW?

- Experts believe the English Setter's ancestors include the Spanish Pointer, large Water Spaniel, and Spring Spaniel.

- The American Kennel Club recognized the English Setter in 1884.

- Show dogs have wavier, longer coats than field dogs.

- The English Setter is the smallest of the three Setter breeds.

COLOR:
White and black, white and orange

COAT:
Flat, silky

ENGLISH SPRINGER SPANIEL

HISTORY

A hunting dog that simultaneously makes a family friend, the English Springer Spaniel is an intelligent, trainable breed that craves companionship. This is a family dog, and the English Springer Spaniel loves people. He's curious, friendly, and can live in large country homes or small city apartments.

Before the development of the rifle, the English Springer Spaniel was a prized asset among game hunters thanks to its ability to 'spring' birds from cover. Once the rifle became increasingly common, the dog cemented its reputation as a gundog.

Recognized as an official breed in the early 20th century, the English Springer Spaniel enjoys the outdoors and thus requires weekly grooming. Its thick, feathery coat can easily become quite dirty, and regular trimming is essential. The breed remains one of the most popular in the United States.

16

CHARACTERISTICS

HEIGHT:
20 inches (male);
19 inches (female)

WEIGHT:
50 pounds (male);
40 pounds (female)

LIFE EXPECTANCY:
12-14 years

GROUP:
Sporting Group

DID YOU KNOW?

- The English Springer Spaniel's acute sense of smell helps authorities identify the smallest traces of explosives.

- Political figures like George W. Bush and George H.W. Bush and celebrities like Oprah Winfrey were all English Springer Spaniel owners.

- Sixteenth century paintings depict dogs that look similiar to the English Springer Spaniel.

- Historians believe that famous Scottish army commander William Wallace owned a dog that was an ancestor of the breed.

COLOR:
Black, white, liver

COAT:
Flat, wavy
(outercoat);
short, soft, dense
(undercoat)

GOLDEN RETRIEVER

HISTORY

Arguably the most popular breed in the United States, the Golden Retriever is a lively, loyal, and playful dog that enjoys the outdoors and daily exercise. The breed is used in hunting, field trials, obedience, and as a guide to the vision-impaired. It is also a therapy dog that can provide comfort to children and the elderly.

One can trace the Golden's roots back to the Scottish Highlands by way of Dudley Marjoribanks, the first Lord Tweedmouth. Tweedmouth crossed his yellow retriever with the now-extinct Tweed Water Spaniel.

The Golden is above all a family dog, easy to train, and outgoing. Their puppyish, joyous behavior lasts well into adulthood.

CHARACTERISTICS

HEIGHT:
**23-24 inches (male);
21.5-22.5 inches (female)**

WEIGHT:
**65-75 pounds (male);
55-65 pounds (female)**

LIFE EXPECTANCY:
10-12 years

GROUP:
Sporting Group

DID YOU KNOW?

- President Gerald Ford owned a female Golden named Liberty. Liberty gave birth to a litter of pups in the White House on September 14, 1975.

- Soft enough for an egg? Yes, it's true: the Golden's mouth is so soft that he can carry a raw egg without cracking the shell.

- Golden Retrievers enjoy few things as much as a meal—or meals. They are prone to overeating, so owners must be diligent about watching portion sizes and limiting treats.

- Golden Retrievers love to please, making obedience training not only a must but also a breeze.

COLOR:
Shades of gold or cream

COAT:
Dense, firm, straight

IRISH SETTER

HISTORY

Like the English Setter, the Irish Setter is a gundog known for its acute sense of smell. The breed was created in the 1700s; its ancestors likely include the English Setter, the Gordon Setter, the Irish Water Spaniel, and other spaniels and pointers.

Irish hunters used the dog to hunt along the green countryside throughout the 1800s, and by the 1870s, the breed gained fame in the show ring. The Irish Setter's popularity grew by the mid-20th century thanks, in part, to President Richard Nixon's Irish Setter named King Timahoe.

This photogenic breed is excellent around children and other pets. Daily exercise and early training are essential.

CHARACTERISTICS

HEIGHT:
27 inches (male);
25 inches (female)

WEIGHT:
70 pounds (male);
60 pounds (female)

LIFE EXPECTANCY:
12-15 years

GROUP:
Sporting Group

DID YOU KNOW?

- The Irish Setter's earliest ancestors were red and white in color, rather than purely red.

- Big Red, the hero of Jim Kjelgaard's 1945 novel of the same name, features arguably the most famous Irish Setter of all time. The book was later adapted into a 1962 Disney film.

- Elcho, the first Irish Setter imported to the United States, arrived in 1875 and became a star show dog.

- The American Kennel Club recognized the breed in 1878.

COLOR:
Red, chestnut

COAT:
Long, silky

IRISH WATER SPANIEL

HISTORY

The tallest of the spaniels, the Irish Water Spaniel is an ideal hiking companion thanks in part to its naturally water-repellent coat and its penchant for ice-cold water.

The breed appeared in Ireland in the 1830s, likely from such ancestors as French Barbet or Poodle-like dogs or perhaps Portuguese Water Dogs. Four Irish Water Spaniels entered the first Westminster Kennel Club show in 1877. To this day, the breed remains much more popular in Ireland than in America.

First-time dog owners, be warned: this breed is notoriously headstrong and requires thorough training at a young age. Adequate brushing is also essential due to the dog's debris-attracting, oily coat.

CHARACTERISTICS

HEIGHT:
**22-24 inches (male);
21-23 inches (female)**

WEIGHT:
**55-68 pounds (male);
45-58 pounds (female)**

LIFE EXPECTANCY:
12-13 years

GROUP:
Sporting Group

DID YOU KNOW?

- In the late 1100s, Irish Water Spaniels were known as Shannon Spaniels, Rat-Tail Spaniels, and Whip-Tail Spaniels.

- The Irish Water Spaniel is perceived as the clownish spaniel due to its exuberant personality and unusual hairdo.

- The American Kennel Club recognized the bred in 1884.

- Boatswain, likely the first modern Irish Water Spaniel, lived from 1834 to 1852.

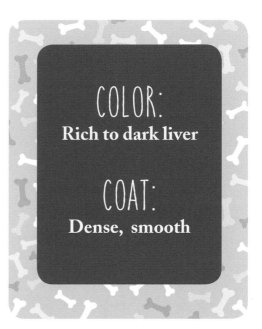

COLOR:
Rich to dark liver

COAT:
Dense, smooth

LABRADOR RETRIEVER

HISTORY

America's most popular dog breed, according to the American Kennel Club, the Labrador Retriever is a high-energy, family-friendly dog that enjoys long walks and bodies of water. This outgoing breed is known for its even temperament, trainability, and need to please.

The Labrador Retriever descended from the Canadian island of Newfoundland. The breed gained popularity in the early 1800s when they were identified by English nobles. The nobles returned to England with the dogs and refined the breed into what is known today as the modern Labrador Retriever.

The breed's round and thick "otter tail" moves back and forth as the dog swims, and the Labrador Retriever's weather-resistant coat is vital for the frigid North Atlantic waters. With its overindulgent appetite, the Labrador Retriever can quickly become obese, so owners of this breed will need to portion meals and schedule plenty of time for play.

CHARACTERISTICS

HEIGHT:
**22.5-24.5 inches (male);
21.5-23.5 inches (female)**

WEIGHT:
**65-80 pounds (male);
55-70 pounds (female)**

LIFE EXPECTANCY:
10-12 years

GROUP:
Sporting Group

DID YOU KNOW?

- The Labrador Retriever is an incredibly popular breed for guide and rescue work.

- Many people mistakenly assume the Labrador Retriever originated from the Labrador region of the Canadian province of Newfoundland and Labrador.

- The American Kennel Club registered its first Labrador Retriever in 1917.

- The breed was originally called St. John's dogs after Newfoundland's capital city.

COLOR:
Black, chocolate, yellow

COAT:
Short, dense

GERMAN SHORTHAIRED POINTER

HISTORY

This popular all-purpose gundog thrives off of companionship, exercise, and a good hunt.

The German Shorthaired Pointer dates back to the 17th century; modern German Shorthaired Pointers evolved in the second half of the 19th century. The German Shorthair's popularity within the United States grew significantly in the mid-20th century. Today, the breed is one of the most popular hunting dogs in the world.

Early and rigorous training is key for the German Shorthair; other family pets, like cats or small animals, could otherwise appear as appetizing prey. German Shorthairs will readily bark at strangers and nosies and act shy around strangers. Owners of this breed should anticipate scheduling about an hour of off-leash exercise per day, for restless German Shorthairs can exhibit destructive behavior.

CHARACTERISTICS

HEIGHT:
**23-25 inches (male);
21-23 inches (female)**

WEIGHT:
**55-70 pounds (male);
46-60 pounds (female)**

LIFE EXPECTANCY:
10-12 years

GROUP:
Sporting Group

DID YOU KNOW?

- The breed has made appearances in books by writers like Robert B. Parker and Rick Bass.

- German Shorthairs won Best in Show at the Westminster Kennel Club Dog Show in 1974 and 2005.

- Prince Albrecht zu Solms-Braunfels of Germany played a key role in the German Shorthair's development.

- Montana's Dr. Charles Thornton imported the first German Shorthair to the United States in 1925.

COLOR:
**Liver roan,
dark brown,
liver and white,
white and chocolate**

COAT:
Short, flat, dense

VIZSLA

HISTORY

A multipurpose dog with a long ancestral legacy, the Vizsla is a hardworking breed that hunts, tracks, and retrieves. It has a sensitive nose and is extremely trainable. The Vizsla is also an exceptional family dog that manages well around children.

Magyar hunters likely used the breed's ancestors as hunters, as millennium-old stone carvings show the ancient people with dogs similar to the Vizsla. The breed would ultimately became immensely popular among Hungarian aristocracy.

The Vizsla is prone to suffering major separation anxiety, so consistent companionship is a must. Like any sporting breed, the Vizsla requires plenty of exercise to release pent-up energy and prevent destructive behavior. Consider challenging the breed with puzzle-oriented games that utilize the Vizsla's intelligence.

CHARACTERISTICS

HEIGHT:
**22-24 inches (male);
21-23 inches (female)**

WEIGHT:
**55-60 pounds (male);
44-55 pounds (female)**

LIFE EXPECTANCY:
12-14 years

GROUP:
Sporting Group

DID YOU KNOW?

- The Vizsla was nearly extinct at the end of World War II.

- A U.S. State Department employee helped smuggle a Vizsla out of Hungary in 1950. It was then brought to America, a first for the breed.

- The breed is the second smallest hunting dog after the Brittany.

- The Vizsla is also known as the Hungarian Pointer.

COLOR:
Golden-rust

COAT:
Short, smooth, dense

WEIMARANER

HISTORY

An intelligent, powerful dog that's descended from various German hunting breeds, the Weimaraner is an energetic gundog that makes for a reliable family member and exercise companion. This sleek breed, with its unusual grayish color, is known for its stealthy movements in the field.

The Weimaraner is a relatively young breed. Developed in the early 1800s, the Weimaraner traces its heritage to Germany's Grand Duke Karl August. The duke longed to develop a hunting dog, and experts say the nobleman crossed Bloodhounds with other European hunting dogs. After first helping to pursue big game animals, the Weimaraner would ultimately be used to retrieve birds from land and water.

This breed requires plenty of physical and mental exercise. It's also an escape artist, so owners should have sturdy gates or fences on their properties. Because this people-centric breed is also prone to suffering from separation anxiety, crate training is recommended.

CHARACTERISTICS

HEIGHT:
**25-27 inches (male);
23-25 inches (female)**

WEIGHT:
**70-90 pounds (male);
55-75 pounds (female)**

LIFE EXPECTANCY:
10-13 years

GROUP:
Sporting Group

DID YOU KNOW?

- The Weimaraner first arrived in the United States in the late 1920s.

- Artist William Wegman famously used Weimaraners in his photographs and videos. Some of those video segments appeared on *Sesame Street*.

- President Dwight D. Eisenhower had a Weimaraner named Heidi.

- The American Kennel Club officially recognized the breed in 1942.

COLOR:
Charcoal-blue, silver-grey, blue-grey

COAT:
Short, hard, smooth

AKITA

HISTORY

The burly, muscular Akita is a loyal family dog that's a national treasure in Japan. The breed is descended from hunting dogs bred in the Akita Prefecture, located on the northwestern edge of Japan's main island.

The breed, or Akita Inu, was first developed in the early 17th century. A banished nobleman, ordered to live out his life on the prefecture, encouraged barons to develop a powerful hunting dog. Subsequent generations of breeding produced the modern Akita.

This is a demanding breed, and it's not encouraged for first-time dog owners. Challenging to train, the Akita requires daily exercise, sheds heavily, and act territorial around other animals. The Akita demands respect and seeks to cut his own path. Early socialization is essential with this breed.

CHARACTERISTICS

HEIGHT:
**26-28 inches (male);
24-26 inches (female)**

WEIGHT:
**100-130 pounds (male);
70-100 pounds (female)**

LIFE EXPECTANCY:
10-13 years

GROUP:
Working Group

DID YOU KNOW?

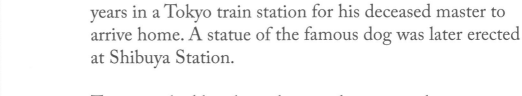

- Hachiko, the most famous Akita of all time, waited nine years in a Tokyo train station for his deceased master to arrive home. A statue of the famous dog was later erected at Shibuya Station.

- Taro, a male Akita brought into the country by a military officer, was the first Akita to be registered in the United States.

- After a Japanese child is born, the family typically receives a small statue of an Akita. The statue signifies happiness, health, and longevity.

- The Akita eanred American Kennel Club recognition in 1972.

COLOR:
Brindle, red, fawn, pure white,

COAT:
Thick, soft, dense (undercoat); straight, harsh (outercoat)

ALASKAN MALAMUTE

HISTORY

The boisterous Alaskan Malamute is an expert Arctic sledge dog that has extraordinary stamina and strength. This powerful dog, after all, was bred to pull sleds and withstand unforgiving temperatures across challenging terrains. Named after an Inuit tribe from Alaska's Kotzebue Sound region, the Alaskan Malamute is one of the world's most ancient breeds.

The 1896 Klondike Gold Rush drew an influx of Alaskan dogs, and prospectors paid large sums for teams of Alaskan Malamutes. During World War I, hundreds of Alaskan Malamutes delivered supplies to French army troops in mountain outposts. In World War II, due to a demand for sled dogs, Alaskan Malamutes were loaned for the war; many were later killed in an Antarctica expedition.

This reliable family dog is friendly around both children and adults. It requires copious amounts of exercise and room to roam. The breed may consider smaller animals as potential prey, so early socialization around other pets is essential. Alaskan Malamutes also love to dig, so providing the breed with a designated digging location is a fine idea.

CHARACTERISTICS

HEIGHT:
25 inches (male);
23 inches (female)

WEIGHT:
85 pounds (male);
75 pounds (female)

LIFE EXPECTANCY:
10-14 years

GROUP:
Working Group

DID YOU KNOW?

- Alaskan Malamutes rarely bark. They do, however, make howling sounds and other low noises.

- The American Kennel Club recognized the Alaskan Malamute in 1935.

- Experts say the breed and humans developed a close relationship, in part, because babies would suckle on dogs alongside puppies.

- Because Alaskan Malamutes greet everyone as a friend, they do not make for reliable watchdogs.

COLOR:
Light gray, black, sable, red

COAT:
Thick, coarse

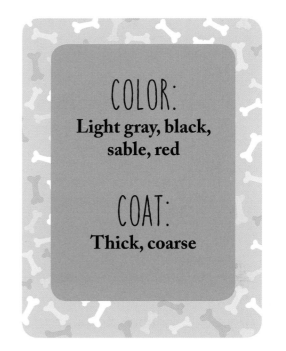

BERNESE MOUNTAIN DOG

HISTORY

The kind, strong, and versatile Bernese Mountain Dog is a hardworking and friendly Mastiff-type dog with Swiss roots. The breed's name derives from Bern, a Swiss canton, where the dog pulled carts, drove livestock to fields, and acted as a watchdog. Today, the Bernese Mountain Dog, or Berner, makes for an excellent family companion thanks to its gentle personality. Besides being a friendly addition to families, the Berner is also an expert therapy dog for the elderly, sick, and people with special needs.

The breed's ancestors were brought into Switzerland more than 2,000 years ago by Roman soldiers. For generations, the Berner was a reliable farmhand that, most notably, could pull carts many times its weight. By the end of the 19th century, however, the breed's population declined significantly, but breeders helped reverse the trend by the early 20th century.

CHARACTERISTICS

HEIGHT:

25-27.5 inches (male);
23-26 inches (female)

WEIGHT:

80-115 pounds (male);
70-95 pounds (female)

LIFE EXPECTANCY:

7-10 years

GROUP:

Working Group

Owners should know that this breed sheds heavily, and, because of its genetic makeup, is prone to a variety of health problems and shorter lifespans. And, because of its size, the breed can accidentally knock over small children. The Berner also requires plenty of shade and water due to its large frame and heavy coat.

DID YOU KNOW?

- The Berner is one of four varieties of Swiss Mountain Dog.

- Because villagers used Berners to transport milk and cheese from mountains to valleys, the breed earned the moniker "Cheese Dog."

- A Kansas farmer imported the first pair of Berners to America in 1926.

- The American Kennel Club recognized the breed in 1937.

COLOR:
Tricolor,
(black, rust
and white)

COAT:
Thick, wavy
or sraight

BOXER

HISTORY

Descended from the war dogs of the
Assyrian empire, the Boxer is a loyal, energetic, and intelligent dog. Slow to mature,
this breed requires thorough training at an
early age. This obedient dog requires a calm
demeanor and leadership.

The Boxer's earlier ancestors were used in
medieval times as a dependable big-game
hunter. These ancestors were found in 16th
and 17th century tapestries and were known
as Bullenbeissers (German for "bull biter").
The Boxer as known today can be traced back
to the late 1800s and early 1900s.

The Boxer make for a fine watchdog, rescue
dog, guide dog, or cattle dog. They also snore
loudly and drool heavily. This dog, like any
working breed, needs plenty of daily exercise
and, if possible, an open space or yard for
play. And don't let children be intimidated
by the Boxer's size, for this breed is friendly
around young ones. Early socialization is
also key around other pets; without it, the
Boxer may employ its hunting instincts.

CHARACTERISTICS

HEIGHT:
**23-25 inches (male);
21.5-23.5 inches (female)**

WEIGHT:
**65-80 pounds (male);
55-70 pounds (female)**

LIFE EXPECTANCY:
10-12 years

GROUP:
Working Group

DID YOU KNOW?

- The breed earned its name based upon the breed's prizefighting way of sparring.

- The Boxer was one of Germany's first breeds selected for police training.

- The American Kennel Club registered its first Boxer in 1904.

- The Boxer consistently ranks as one of America's most popular breeds.

COLOR:
Gold, black brindle

COAT:
Short, shiny, smooth

CANE CORSO

HISTORY

Hailing from southern Italy, the Cane Corso is a graceful tracking and guard dog that's plenty intelligent and robust. This giant breed is headstrong, large, and has a strong prey drive. The Cane Corso likes to work and receive serious companionship from his family.

Experts believe the Cane Corso is descended from Roman war dogs. The breed was bred to guard property, hunt, and work on farmland. After a decline in the Industrial Revolution, the Cane Corso received a resurgence throughout the second half of the 20th century.

This Mastiff-type breed is not recommended for first-time dog owners; a responsible, experienced owner is paramount to care for this breed. Training must begin as soon as a puppy is brought home, and obedience class is a must. Daily walks and play are also key for a healthy Cane Corso. This breed is incredibly useful on a ranch or farm but is also a great fit for dog sports or activities that give the dog mental and physical stimulation.

CHARACTERISTICS

HEIGHT:
**25-27.5 inches (male);
23.5-26 inches (female)**

WEIGHT:
88-110 pounds

LIFE EXPECTANCY:
9-12 years

GROUP:
Working Group

DID YOU KNOW?

- The first litter of Cane Corsos was imported to the United States in 1988.

- The Cane Corso is known as Dogo di Puglia, which means "dog of Puglia."

- The American Kennel Club recognized the breed in 2010.

- The breed neared extinction during World War II.

COLOR:
Black, gray, fawn, red

COAT:
Short, shiny, stiff

DOBERMAN PINSCHER

HISTORY

Agile, sleek, and strong, the Doberman Pinscher is a protective breed that's an equally reliable police and house dog. This breed is incredibly easy to train, and while it requires a rigid approach to instruction, the Doberman offers obedience and loyalty. It's also very intelligent and requires plenty of attention and stimulation.

Karl Friedrich Louis Doberman, a German tax official, developed the breed in the late 1800s in an effort to create a dog for protection. The breed's popularity dropped during World War I and again in World War II. Luckily, Dobermans were brought to the United States throughout this time, a move credited by some as essential to the breed's survival.

The Doberman's ancestors include the German Shepherd Dog, German Pinscher, and possibly the Greyhound, Rottweiler, the Manchester Terrier, and the Weimaraner.

This is a family dog that despises being left alone; he should live indoors and not in the backyard. The Doberman enjoys living with the family, physically and mentally. He's also no fan of cold weather.

CHARACTERISTICS

HEIGHT:
26-28 inches (male);
24-26 inches (female)

WEIGHT:
75-100 pounds (male);
60-90 pounds (female)

LIFE EXPECTANCY:
10-12 years

GROUP:
Working Group

COLOR:
Red, black,
Isabella, blue

COAT:
Smooth, short,
thick

DID YOU KNOW?

- The Doberman was a popular dog in the U.S. Marine Corps in World War II. The dogs were nicknamed "devil dogs."

- The first Doberman to win Best in Show at the Westminster Kennel Club Dog Show was in 1939.

- A life-size statue of a Doberman named "Always Faithful" stands at the war dog cemetery in Guam. The monument commemorates the 25 dogs that died liberating the island in World War II.

- The Doberman excels at agility and obedience tests and competitions.

GREAT DANE

HISTORY

Fear not: this massive dog is a gentle giant. The Great Dane, or the "Apollo of Dogs," is a people-pleasing breed that makes for a lovable family dog. The Great Dane is easy to groom, content with about 20 minutes of exercise per day, and has a desire to please.

The Great Dane is an old breed. In fact, the oldest written description of dog akin to the gentle giant possibly dates back to 1121 B.C. In later years, German nobles used the sprawling breed to hunt wild boars and as an estate watchdog. It's unclear when the Great Dane arrived in the United States, though it was likely sometime in the later half of the 19th century.

Because of its sheer size, the Great Dane is prone to producing massive amounts of slobber. The breed makes for a fine house dog so long as there is abundant room for the dog to roam. Great Dane puppies must not be permitted to run or jump much, for their growing bones and joints could become damaged. Prospective owners should also remember that, with such a large dog, costs for veterinary care, food, and other expenses can easily run high.

CHARACTERISTICS

HEIGHT:
30-32 inches (male);
28-30 inches (female)

WEIGHT:
140-175 pounds (male);
110-140 pounds (female)

LIFE EXPECTANCY:
7-10 years

GROUP:
Working Group

DID YOU KNOW?

- A Great Dane named Zeus held the 2012 Guinness World Record as the tallest dog in the world at 44 inches.

- Despite its name, the Great Dane has no known connection to Denmark.

- Scooby Doo, arguably the most famous Great Dane in popular culture, is the hero of the famous television series that premiered in 1969.

- Regardless of its mammoth frame, the Great Dane is an apartment-friendly dog. But owners should remain cognizant about its size, especially if the dog is ill and cannot walk.

COLOR:
Blue, black, brindle

COAT:
Short, thick

GREAT PYRENEES

HISTORY

The powerful, large, and patient Great Pyrenees is a mountain dog and a mellow companion. Its striking white coat no doubt contributes to its folklorish majesty. This courageous yet calm breed requires a plethora of socialization and training at a young age, for its large size will otherwise make it an almost impossible living companion. But diligent owners will receive in return an affectionate and devoted breed.

The breed's roots can be traced to France's Pyrenees Mountains. There, the guard dog protected flocks from wolves and other intrusive animals. The Great Pyrenees was also a guard dog for noble figures like King Louis XIV. The breed arrived to the United States in the 19th century, and the American Kennel Club recognized the Great Pyrenees in 1933.

With its tolerant and patient personality, the Great Pyrenees is excellent around children. But like any dog its size, this breed requires substantial training at a very early age. Socialization, exposure, and obedience classes are extremely important. Future owners should also know that the breed has a penchant for barking thanks to its superb hearing.

CHARACTERISTICS

HEIGHT:
27-32 inches (male);
25-29 inches (female)

WEIGHT:
More than 100 pounds (male);
More than 85 pounds (female)

LIFE EXPECTANCY:
10-12 years

GROUP:
Working Group

DID YOU KNOW?

- Like the Great Dane, the Great Pyrenees can live in apartments. But owners should remain mindful about its large size.

- The breed's nickname in France is Patou, which means shepherd.

- The first Great Pyrenees was brought to the United States in 1824.

- Remains of the breed are found in Bronze Age fossil deposits.

COLOR:
White, gray, badger, reddish brown, tan

COAT:
Long, thick, coarse, dense, woolly

GREATER SWISS MOUNTAIN DOG

HISTORY

A powerful, big-boned breed, the Greater Swiss Mountain Dog (or Swissy) is a confident dog that requires an abundance of training, socialization, and homework. Once trained, however, the breed is a fine family companion, often gentle, and a reliable watchdog. Famous for its tricolor coat, the Swissy is an altogether agile dog that requires moderate levels of exercise and a fenced yard.

Descended from the mastiff-type dogs of the Romans, the Swissy was used for cart pulling, property guarding, and herding. During industrialization, however, the breed nearly died out. Luckily, the Swissy saw a resurgence in the early 20th century.

The Swissy can easily overheat, so air conditioning or fans are a must during hot weather (as is fresh water). The breed also requires an authority figure or household leader. The Swissy may also chase other animals, and even small children, so this behavior must be curtailed at a young age.

CHARACTERISTICS

HEIGHT:
25.5-28.5 inches (male);
23.5-27 inches (female)

WEIGHT:
115-140 pounds (male);
85-110 pounds (female)

LIFE EXPECTANCY:
8-11 years

GROUP:
Working Group

DID YOU KNOW?

- The first Swissy imported to the United States was in 1968.

- Famous dog expert Albert Heim revived the breed in the early 20th century.

- The Swissy is related to the Bernese Mountain Dog.

- The American Kennel Club recognized the Swissy in 1995.

COLOR:
Black, rich rust, white

COAT:
Dense, thick

KOMONDOR

HISTORY

Despite his admittedly goofy appearance, the Komondor is a dependable breed with a rich history. This working dog hails from Hungary and spent centuries guarding flocks and fighting off hungry predators. Today, most Komondors spend their days as a family companion.

Experts believe the Komondor arrived in Hungary about a millennium ago with Magyar nomads. The Komondor neared extinction at the end of World War II, and following the end of imports from Hungary during the Cold War, the breed suffered mightily. Luckily, the Komondor's numbers rebounded during the second half of the 20th century.

Prospective Komondor owners, be warned: this is not a breed for new dog owners. The Komondor's size, independence, smarts, and aggressiveness around other dogs can make for a challenging experience. But those with the experience and patience to train this dog will find that the breed makes for a rewarding family friend.

CHARACTERISTICS

HEIGHT:
**27.5 inches and up (male);
25.5 inches and up (female)**

WEIGHT:
**More than 100 pounds (male);
More than 80 pounds (female)**

LIFE EXPECTANCY:
10-12 years

GROUP:
Working Group

DID YOU KNOW?

- The Komdondor is a direct descendant of the Russian herdsman's dog Aftscharka.

- The Komondor's cords, which develop around age two, help camouflage the breed with sheep and shield it from predators.

- The American Kennel Club recognized the Komondor in 1937.

- Komondor puppies take about three years to reach maturity.

COLOR:
White

COAT:
Dense, wooly, curly

51

MASTIFF

HISTORY

The mammoth Mastiff is a gentle yet protective breed that is of ancient origin. Descended from the Molosser, Mastiff-type dogs served for centuries as guards and fighters. Once war dogs, the Mastiff has a more friendly reputation today as a loyal family member.

The modern Mastiff was developed in England. After near-extinction in the first half of the 19th century, the breed rebounded thanks, in part, to the Mastiff's reputation as a show dog. It's unclear precisely when the breed arrived in the United States, but the first Mastiff club in the country was formed in 1879. The American Kennel Club recognized the breed in 1885.

Mastiffs are prone to producing lots of slobber and passing massive amounts of gas. But outside of his large size, the Mastiff is a relatively easy dog to share a home with. He's a peaceful breed that can easily sense threats. The breed can live in apartments, but owners whose homes have stairs should be realistic about how they will move the dog should he become incapacitated.

CHARACTERISTICS

HEIGHT:
**30 inches and up (male);
27.5 inches and up (female)**

WEIGHT:
**160-230 pounds (male);
120-170 pounds (female)**

LIFE EXPECTANCY:
6-10 years

GROUP:
Working Group

DID YOU KNOW?

- Mastiffs were described in Julius Caesar's account of the 55 B.C. invasion of Britain.

- Mastiffs fought alongside the British in the 1415 Battle of Agincourt against the French.

- Chaucer called the breed "Alaunts" in his famous *Canterbury Tales*.

- An estimated 14 Mastiffs survived in England at the end of World War II.

COLOR:
Fawn, apricot, or brindle

COAT:
Straight, coarse, short

NEWFOUNDLAND

HISTORY

The patient, child-friendly Newfoundland is a brilliant water dog that's capable of strenuous work. A strong swimmer and laborer, this breed is also friendly, kind, and protective. But because of his large size, the Newfoundland is prone to orthopedic health problems.

The Newfoundland's ancestry is obscure. Some experts believe the breed descended from the Great Pyrenees, while others suggest its ancestors may be the French Boarhound or a Nordic breed. Regardless, today's Newfoundland derived from eastern Canada. That's where the breed assisted fishermen, saved shipwreck victims, and pulled carts.

Early socialization is a must for the Newfoundland. Owners should be cautious about excessively exercising Newfoundland puppies, for too much activity could damage the dog's growth plates. This breed is also a lifelong drooler, so owners should be comfortable with cleaning up after their four-legged companion.

COLOR:
Black, brown, gray, white

COAT:
Flat, water-resistant, coarse

CHARACTERISTICS

HEIGHT:
28 inches (male);
26 inches (female)

WEIGHT:
130-150 pounds (male);
100-120 pounds (female)

LIFE EXPECTANCY:
9-10 years

GROUP:
Working Group

DID YOU KNOW?

- President James Buchanan's Newfoundland, Lara, was a popular addition to the White House.

- A newfoundland named Seaman was part of Lewis and Clark's monumental 1802 trek across America. He stands today in 10 separate Lewis and Clark monuments throughout the United States.

- The breed was nearly wiped out in the 1780s.

- Robert Kennedy's family owned a Newfoundland named Brumus.

PORTUGUESE WATER DOG

HISTORY

Intelligent, energetic, and hypoallergenic, the Portuguese Water Dog was once a staple of Portugal's coast where it herded fish, sent messages between boats, and retrieved nets. The breed is also notable for its webbed feet. Technology advancements ultimately made the dog unemployable, but the breed's popularity grew once again in the second half of the 20th century once it was brought to the United States.

Experts say evidence of the breed can be traced to pre-Christian years. Written descriptions of the Portuguese Water Dog date back to 1297. The breed most likely shares an ancestor with the Poodle, Irish Water Spaniel, and Kerry Blue Terrier.

The Portuguese Water Dog makes for a superb family dog, as this breed is excellent around children. This breed does poorly if left alone. Training and socialization should begin at a young age. Owners who dislike their dog getting wet should steer clear of this breed.

CHARACTERISTICS

HEIGHT:
20-23 inches (male);
17-21 inches (female)

WEIGHT:
42-60 pounds (male);
35-50 pounds (female)

LIFE EXPECTANCY:
11-13 years

GROUP:
Working Group

DID YOU KNOW?

- Two Portuguese Water Dogs, Bo and Sunny, occupied President Barack Obama's White House.

- The breed is known in Portugal as Cão de Água, which translates to "dog of the water."

- Portuguese shipping magnate Vasco Bensuade is credited with saving the breed in the early 20th century.

- The American Kennel Club recognized the breed in 1984.

COLOR:
Black, white, brown

COAT:
Profuse, thick

ROTTWEILER

HISTORY

With its Roman Mastiff roots, the Rottweiler is a powerful breed that requires an abundance of socialization and training at an early age. He can be aggressive around other dogs, and he certainly has a strong prey drive, but the Rottweiler is typically a superb family pet. Despite their often negative persona, Rottweilers are a loyal and hardworking breed.

For centuries, the Rottweiler was a popular cattle, hunting, and cart pulling breed. By the end of the 19th century, the breed nearly died out but was revived in the early 20th century. Over the past 100 years, the Rottweiler has become a popular police, rescue, and guard dog.

The Rottweiler is most likely not an ideal dog for first-time owners. This is a muscular dog that often displays independent thinking. What a Rottweiler might consider to be a simple nudge may be for some, especially the young and old, an aggressive action. Still, with proper training, this breed can easily become an excellent family companion.

CHARACTERISTICS

HEIGHT:
24-27 inches (male);
22-25 inches (female)

WEIGHT:
95-135 pounds (male);
80-100 pounds (female)

LIFE EXPECTANCY:
9-10 years

GROUP:
Working Group

DID YOU KNOW?

- The first German breed standard was created in 1901.

- The first Rottweiler likely came to the United States in the late 1920s.

- More than 100,000 Rottweilers were registered with the American Kennel Club in the late 20th century.

- The Rottweiler was one of the first guide dogs for the blind.

COLOR:
Black, rust

COAT:
Straight, coarse, dense

SAINT BERNARD

HISTORY

The giant Saint Bernard is a powerful Mastiff-type breed that drools, has a sensitivity to heat, and needs manageable amounts of exercise. The breed is also gentle, patient, and enjoys accompanying people. The Saint Bernard is excellent around children, but due to his size, supervision is essential around younger kids.

Monks of the Swiss Alps-based St. Bernard's Hospice developed the Saint Bernard over hundreds of years. The dog helped rescue struggling travelers from fatigue, avalanches, and disorientation. The breed's numbers dropped very low in the early 19th century; crosses were later made with the Newfoundland. Later on in the century, Saint Bernards became popular in places outside of Switzerland like England.

Prospective owners should know that the breed requires plenty of space, water, and food; because of these facts, the Saint Bernard is not suitable for apartments or small spaces. The breed is moderately active and should not live outdoors. The Saint Bernard also excels in dog sports, including cart pulling and obedience trials.

CHARACTERISTICS

HEIGHT:
**28-30 inches (male);
26-28 inches (female)**

WEIGHT:
**140-180 pounds (male);
120-140 pounds (female)**

LIFE EXPECTANCY:
8-10 years

GROUP:
Working Group

DID YOU KNOW?

- Saint Bernards have also been known as Sacred Dogs, Alpine Mastiffs, Barryhunden, and Alpendogs.

- The most famous St. Bernard's Hospice rescue dog, Barry, reportedly rescued more than 40 people in the early 1800s.

- Contrary to popular belief, Saint Bernards did not carry casks of medicinal brandy around their necks.

- Saint Bernards were shorthaired before 1830.

COLOR:
Brindle

COAT:
Dense, short, tough

SAMOYED

HISTORY

Cheerful, graceful, and tireless, the Samoyed is a smart and sociable breed that makes for a loving family companion. The Samoyed's striking white coat requires a hefty amount of weekly grooming, and he can be stubborn and exhibit a penchant for barking. But, with the right family, this magnificent breed can easily make for a wonderful friend.

This ancient breed was once the companion of the nomadic Samoyede, a group of people who arrived in Siberia a millennium ago. The Samoyed acclimated to extremely cold temperatures as it helped herd reindeer, haul sledges, and hunt. Centuries later, Samoyeds took part in Sir Ernest Shackleton's Antarctic exploration. The American Kennel Club recognized the breed in 1906.

The Samoyed craves relationships; a lonely Samoyed is a destructive Samoyed. Owners should curtail any barking problems at a young age. The Samoyed also has a serious prey drive, so training and a well-built fence are necessary. This breed requires almost daily grooming to maintain its brilliant coat.

CHARACTERISTICS

HEIGHT:
21-23.5 inches (male);
19-21 inches (female)

WEIGHT:
45-65 pounds (male);
35-50 pounds (female)

LIFE EXPECTANCY:
12-14 years

GROUP:
Working Group

DID YOU KNOW?

- The correct pronunciation is "Sam-a-YED."

- Because its mouth curves up at the corners, the Samoyed is not a drooler.

- The Samoyed's shedding hair can easily become a garment.

- The Samoyed is an agile breed that is a serious competitor in dog sports.

COLOR:
White

COAT:
Heavy, soft, thick

SIBERIAN HUSKY

HISTORY

Happy, sociable, and versatile, the Siberian Husky is an independent thinker with a pack instinct. Known for its well-furred coat and erect, high-set ears, this breed originates from northeastern Asia where it served as a companion to the Chukchi people as well as a sled dog. This is a high-energy breed that can be destructive if isolated and left alone.

Outside of its Siberian nomadic origins, much of the Siberian Husky's history remains a mystery. The breed was used as a sled dog in Alaska after it was imported to the state in 1908. The Siberian Husky thrived in the United States throughout the 20th century despite the closing of Siberia's borders in the 1930s.

The Siberian Husky needs plenty of daily exercise. This breed doesn't bark but rather howls; it also loves to dig and sheds year-round. And those with multiple small animals at home, be warned: the Siberian Husky has a serious prey drive, so this breed may not be the best fit. However, this working breed can easily make for a lovable family friend.

CHARACTERISTICS

HEIGHT:
15-18 inches

WEIGHT:
30-45 pounds (male)
25-40 pounds (female)

LIFE EXPECTANCY:
10-14 years

GROUP:
Working Group

DID YOU KNOW?

- Balto, a Siberian Husky, led a team of Siberian Huskies through a dangerous blizzard to deliver diphtheria vaccines to remote Alaska in 1925.

- Siberian Huskies served with the U.S. Army in World War II.

- The American Kennel Club recognized the breed in 1930.

- Siberian Huskies can have different colored eyes.

COLOR:
Any color

COAT:
Soft, dense

BASENJI

HISTORY

The graceful, independent, and alert Basenji is a primitive hunting breed from Central Africa. Used by pygmy hunters, Basenjis have typically lived in a pack alongside tribes. Today, this breed makes for an excellent house dog, thanks in part to its sense of humor, energy, and intelligence.

Experts say Basenjis are one of the most ancient breeds. Some are depicted in Egyptian artifacts and other prehistoric art. A pair of Basenjis was brought to Britain in the late 19th century, though sadly, the dogs died. Decades later, the first Basenjis were successfully imported into western countries. The breed's popularity in the West grew steadily throughout the 20th century.

True to his independent nature, the Basenji might not always obey instructions. Early, consistent training and socialization can help curtail some of this aloof behavior. This breed also loves to explore new things, be it a new park or a heap of trash. And if you're particularly attached to certain possessions, such as shoes, be warned: your Basenji could easily destroy them.

CHARACTERISTICS

HEIGHT:
17 inches (male);
16 inches (female)

WEIGHT:
24 pounds (male);
22 pounds (female)

LIFE EXPECTANCY:
13-14 years

GROUP:
Hound Group

DID YOU KNOW?

- Western explorers in the 1600s described the breed as "Congo Terrier" or "Bush Dog."

- Rather than barking, the Basenji makes yodeling noises.

- The breed exercises some catlike characteristics, such as self-cleaning.

- The American Kennel Club recognized the breed in 1943.

COLOR:
Variety of colors

COAT:
Short, fine

BASSET HOUND

HISTORY

A slow-paced hunting dog that is excellent around kids, the Basset Hound is known for its large, floppy ears and its excellent sense of smell. The breed is a popular family pet that is calm and loyal but is prone to stubbornness; early training and socialization can help create a well-rounded dog.

Originally bred in France and Belgium, the Basset Hound descends from breeds developed in the 7th century. Abbot Hubert developed the breed, which was originally known as St. Hubert hounds. One of the line of breeds was an ancestor of the present-day Bloodhound; a mutation resulted in a short-legged dwarf hound. The Basset Hound would later become popular with the French aristocracy; by the middle of the 19th century, the breed made its way to Britain. The Basset Hound likely made its way to American in colonial times, but the breed was not recognized by the American Kennel Club until 1916.

This is a laid-back breed that derives its greatest excitement from finding a scent. To curb his curiosity from leading to trouble, a well-built fence is seriously recommended. The breed is also a pack dog that enjoys the company of others, be it humans or other animals. And because of its constant shedding, the Basset Hound requires daily brushing.

CHARACTERISTICS

HEIGHT:
13-15 inches

WEIGHT:
45-60 pounds

LIFE EXPECTANCY:
12-13 years

GROUP:
Hound Group

DID YOU KNOW?

- The breed's name derives from the French word bas, which means "low."

- The Basset Hound's nose is the most accurate after the Bloodhound.

- The first recorded mention of the Basset Hound was in a 1585 illustrated hunting book.

- The Basset Hound's long ears help sweep scent particles up from the ground toward the nose.

COLOR:
Variety of colors

COAT:
Hard, smooth, short

BEAGLE

HISTORY

The Beagle is an easygoing, happy-go-lucky hunting dog that's simple to train. An equally popular hunting and companion breed, the Beagle makes for an excellent pet so long as it has plenty of company and a fenced yard. But because of its size, the Beagle is suitable for apartment living.

The ancestry of the Beagle is relatively unknown. By the 16th century, English hunters used Beagle-type dogs to hunt hare and rabbit. The breed arrived in the United States following the Civil War, and following its arrival, the Beagle became a huge hit. Besides a family pet, the Beagle is also a valuable asset to law enforcement, thanks to its ability to sniff out drugs and explosives.

The breed does not droll nor does do it emit a noticeable odor. It does, however, enjoy to bark or bay. Extensive training is required to curtail the breed's penchant for obnoxious levels of noise. Prospective owners should also know that the Beagle is prone to laziness as an adult, so consistent, lifelong exercise is essential for a healthy pet.

CHARACTERISTICS

HEIGHT:
13-15 inches

WEIGHT:
20-30 pounds

LIFE EXPECTANCY:
10-15 years

GROUP:
Hound Group

DID YOU KNOW?

- The American Kennel Club registered its first Beagle in 1885.

- President Lyndon B. Johnson owned three beagles named Edgar, Him and Her.

- Snoopy, the cartoon Beagle in the *Peanuts* comic strip, is arguably the most famous Beagle in the world.

- K-Run's Park Me In First, also known as Uno, was the first Beagle to win Best in Show at the Westminster Kennel Club in 2008.

COLOR:
Variety of colors

COAT:
Hard, sleek

BLOODHOUND

HISTORY

The Bloodhound is an expert tracking dog with a nose so powerful that it's often called a nose with a dog attached. He can trail a scent for days; this dog is by no means lazy. He's gentle, sociable, and independent, but he can also be stubborn.

The Bloodhound is an old breed, and its descendants have been around for centuries. The modern breed descends from the 8th century St. Hubert hound. William the Conqueror brought St. Hubert hounds to England when he conquered the nation in 1066. The Victorians later refined the breed after the Bloodhound neared risk of extinction.

Because of the Bloodhound's absolutely phenomenal nose, owners are encouraged to put their Bloodhound to use, be it a local search and rescue group or another noble endeavor. If not, dog games, especially hide and seek, are fine ways to exercise the dog's acute sense of smell. The breed is highly trainable, especially at a young age. It also has a voracious appetite, so valuable items around the home should be properly stowed away and out of sight.

COLOR:
Black and tan, liver and tan, red

COAT:
Short, hard

CHARACTERISTICS

HEIGHT:
25-27 inches (male);
23-25 inches (female)

WEIGHT:
90-110 pounds (male);
80-100 pounds (female)

LIFE EXPECTANCY:
10-12 years

GROUP:
Hound Group

DID YOU KNOW?

- Sir Robert Boyle, a 17th century scientist, reported a Bloodhound that tracked a man more than seven miles through two towns and all the way to a room.

- Evidence from a Bloodhound is admissible in most courts.

- In 1977, two 14-month-old Bloodhounds tracked down Martin Luther King Jr.'s assassin James Earl Ray after he escaped from prison.

- Queen Victoria entered one of her Bloodhounds into a dog show in 1869.

DACHSHUND

HISTORY

Despite its small size, the Dachshund is a fierce, brave, and bold breed. This protective and loyal hound, known as a "wiener" and "sausage dog," still hunts with some owners, but for many, the Dachshund is a popular family pet. The breed is protective toward its human family, and, despite the Dachshund's small size, this dog requires a plethora of daily mental and physical exercise.

Illustrations resembling the Dachshund date back to the 1500s; writings describing the dog date back to the 1600s. Germans later refined the breed about 300 years ago, and it was developed to hunt prey like badgers, rabbits, fox, and stoat. Today's Dachshund has even shorter legs than their ancestors; the short legs help the dog to pursue prey in small tunnels.

The Dachshund loves to bark, and this small dog has an impressive voice. The breed also loves to eat, and he should certainly not be overfed, as too much weight could translate to skeletal problems. The Dachshund is a generally outgoing and social breed, so excessively shy puppies should be avoided.

CHARACTERISTICS

HEIGHT:
**8-9 inches (standard);
5-6 inches (miniature)**

WEIGHT:
**16-32 pounds (standard);
Up to 11 pounds (miniature)**

LIFE EXPECTANCY:
12-16 years

GROUP:
Hound Group

DID YOU KNOW?

- The name "Dachshund" means "badger dog" in German.

- The American Kennel Club recognizes six different Dachshund breeds: the standard and miniature Dachshund, with the smooth, wire-haired, and longhaired coat types.

- Dachshunds first arrived in the United States in 1870 to hunt rabbits.

- The Dachshund is the only American Kennel Club-recognized breed that hunts both below and above ground.

COLOR:
Variety of colors

COAT:
Smooth, short, shining (Smooth Dachshund); tight, thick, short, rough (Wirehaired Dachshund); sleek, glistening, wavy (Longhaired Dachshund)

GREYHOUND

HISTORY

The fastest breed of dog, the Greyhound is a popular racing dog and family pet. The gentle, athletic breed has a distinctive narrow appearance. It's also quiet, independent, and, perhaps surprisingly, content with small amounts of exercise.

Ancient Egyptian tombs depicted slender hounds like the Greyhound more than 5,000 years ago. Britain's Canute Laws mentioned the Greyhound in 1016 in a passage that declared it a crime for poor people to keep the breed. Spanish explorers later brought the Greyhound to the Americas with much success. Ultimately, the American Kennel Club recognized the Greyhound in 1885.

Track-bred Greyhounds make wonderful pets, primarily because they have a host of social experiences that make them less prone to behavioral problems. However, some Greyhounds, especially track-bred ones, can suffer from severe separation anxiety. Greyhounds also love to chase; the safest thing is to never let a Greyhound off leash in areas without a fence, especially puppies.

CHARACTERISTICS

HEIGHT:
**28-30 inches (male);
27-28 inches (female)**

WEIGHT:
**65-70 pounds (male);
60-65 pounds (female)**

LIFE EXPECTANCY:
10-13 years

GROUP:
Hound Group

DID YOU KNOW?

- Mick the Miller, a popular racing Greyhound from the United Kingdom, won 19 consecutive races and even appeared in a film after his retirement in 1931.

- President Rutherford B. Hayes owned a Greyhound named Grim.

- In short bursts, the Greyhound can reach speeds of 45 miles per hour.

- A 1486 poem in the *Book of Saint Albans* described that a Greyhound should be "headed like a snake and necked like a drake, footed like a cat, tailed like a rat, backed like a beam, (and) sided like a bream."

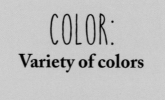

COLOR:
Variety of colors

COAT:
Short, smooth, firm

RHODESIAN RIDGEBACK

HISTORY

The high-strung Rhodesian Ridgeback is an athletic hound native to Zimbabwe. This dog has the stamina to work all day and night, but today, the breed is more likely a household companion. The Ridgeback is, in fact, incredibly protective toward his human family. This breed requires a firm, experienced owner who is willing to provide his dog plenty of physical and mental exercise.

The Ridgeback's ancestors include dogs that European settlers brought to southern Africa in the 1500s and 1600s. South African Boer farmers developed the breed by crossing Great Danes, Mastiffs, Greyhounds, and Bloodhounds. The Ridgeback ultimately helped hunters hunt big game, including lions. The first Ridgeback breed standard was created in 1922.

Despite its muscular appearance, the Ridgeback needs only moderate levels of exercise. He also rarely barks, but he has a serious appetite. Plenty of training and socialization is essential at an early age, particularly to try to curtail the breed's predator instincts. The Ridgeback functions well around children, but it may be too boisterous for toddlers.

CHARACTERISTICS

HEIGHT:
**25-27 inches (male);
24-26 inches (female)**

WEIGHT:
**85 pounds (male);
70 pounds (female)**

LIFE EXPECTANCY:
10-12 years

GROUP:
Hound Group

DID YOU KNOW?

- The Rhodesian Ridgeback is sometimes known as the African Lion Dog, because it's been used to hunt lion with hunters on horseback.

- The American Kennel Club recognized the breed in 1955.

- The Rhodesian Ridgeback has a characteristic ridge of hair down the middle of his back.

- Movie star Errol Flynn bred Ridgebacks on his Hollywood ranch in the 1930s.

COLOR:
Light wheaten to red wheaten

COAT:
Short, dense, sleek

WHIPPET

HISTORY

The graceful, elegant, and gentle Whippet is a sensitive breed that makes for an excellent watchdog. The Whippet rarely barks, it's relatively quiet, and it is loyal toward its human family. It has an odor-free coat, a strong prey drive, and a playful temperament around children. This is an indoor breed that is suitable for apartment living.

Created in the 18th century, the Whippet's ancestors include small Greyhounds and terriers. Whippets hunted small animals and vermin and quickly became a popular sporting dog. The American Kennel Club recognized the breed in 1888.

Whippet puppies can be highly rambunctious; barking, chewing, and digging are daily activities. Eventually, however, puppies will mature into reliably quiet and mellow adults. Whippets also enjoy comfy furniture, so owners should be prepared to share their couch or fireplace chair with their canine friend. And because of their short coat, Whippets easily get cold. A reliable sweater or coat is a fine idea.

CHARACTERISTICS

HEIGHT:
**19-22 inches (male);
18-21 inches (female)**

WEIGHT:
25-40 pounds

LIFE EXPECTANCY:
12-15 years

GROUP:
Hound Group

DID YOU KNOW?

- This fast breed can reach speeds of 35 mph.

- The Whippet earned the moniker "Poor Man's Racehorse" due to the breed's allure among working class families in 1800s England.

- English mill workers who settled in Massachusetts introduced the breed to the United States.

- Experts recommend that Whippet owners with a yard install a 5- to 6-foot fence. Electrical fences do little to deter a Whippet's inherent prey drive.

COLOR:
Any color

COAT:
Short, close, smooth, firm

AUSTRALIAN SHEPHERD

HISTORY

An energetic and intelligent breed, the Australian Shepherd is a tough herding dog that likes to be kept busy. A bored Aussie is a destructive Aussie. This breed loves to chase, compete in dog sports and games, and even 'herd' children. The Aussie requires an abundance of mental and physical stimulation, so prospective owners expecting a mellow breed should expect otherwise.

The Australian Shepherd's ancestry is obscure. Possible Aussie ancestors include Australian Collie-type breeds, German sheepdogs, and other herding dogs. The breed's popularity soared following World War II, after it was featured in movies, rodeos, and television shows. Today, Aussies serve as search and rescue dogs, therapy dogs, drug dogs, and service dogs. The American Kennel Club recognized the Australian Shepherd in 1993.

CHARACTERISTICS

HEIGHT:
**20-23 inches (male);
18-21 inches (female)**

WEIGHT:
**50-65 pounds (male);
40-55 pounds (female)**

LIFE EXPECTANCY:
12-15 years

GROUP:
Herding Group

The Australian Shepherd is not an apartment dog; however, because of its adaptability, it doesn't require a large backyard. It also requires up to an hour of exercise a day. This breed loves to chase, be it cars, small animals, or even small children.

DID YOU KNOW?

- The Australian Shepherd is an excellent running mate.

- Despite its misleading name, the Australian Shepherd is an American-born breed.

- The breed has a range of eye colors, including blue, hazel, green, and amber, as well as different colored eyes.

- The Australian Shepherd has appeared in several Disney films, including *Run, Appaloosa, Run* and *Stub, The Best Cow Dog in the West*.

COLOR:
**Blue merle,
black, red merle**

COAT:
Straight, wavy

BELGIAN MALINOIS

HISTORY

The high-energy Belgian Malinois is an excellent tracking dog and a star among police and military outfits. This shorthaired, agile breed is always alert, and its intelligence makes it an excellent candidate for challenging canine sports or activities. The Belgian Malinois is a confident and outgoing breed with a strong prey drive that may need to be curtailed around other small animals.

The breed began to gain popularity in the late 19th century. Following World War II, the Malinois reemerged in the United States. In 1959, the American Kennel Club separated the Malinois into three separate breeds. Today, the breed has an appearance similar to the German Shepherd.

The Belgian Malinois requires training and socialization at a young age. He thrives best with a sturdy fence, sizable living space, and an experienced owner. He's also excellent around dogs; however, due to the breed's herding instincts, the Malinois may aggressively chase small children.

CHARACTERISTICS

HEIGHT:
**24-26 inches (male);
22-24 inches (female)**

WEIGHT:
**60-80 pounds (male);
40-60 pounds (female)**

LIFE EXPECTANCY:
14-16 years

GROUP:
Hearding Group

DID YOU KNOW?

- The first Belgian Malinois dogs were first brought to America in 1911.

- The breed is known as the Chien de Berger Belge in Europe.

- The Belgian Malinois derived its name from the Belgian city of Malines.

- The U.S. Secret Service uses the Belgian Malinois to guard the White House.

COLOR:
Gray, red

COAT:
Straight, hard

85

BORDER COLLIE

HISTORY

One of the brightest breeds in the world, the whip-smart Border Collie is a remarkably agile dog. This herding dog excels at rounding up sheep (or really anything), performing search and rescue work, and forming close bonds with its human counterparts. The breed is also known for its remarkable ability to concentrate, its independence, and its desire to please.

First classified as the Scotch Sheep Dog, the Border Collie hails from the British Isles. In fact, most Border Collies are descended from a northern England dog named Old Help who was born in 1894. The breed formally earned its name following World War I, and the American Kennel Club recognized the Border Collie in October 1995.

Apartment dwellers should only consider the breed if they maintain a lifestyle as equally active as their canine friend. Like for many breeds, early socialization is essential, for the dog could otherwise become excessively shy or fearful. Border Collies may or may not manage well around other non-canine pets like cats; after all, it's most likely that the dog will attempt to herd other animals.

CHARACTERISTICS

HEIGHT:
**19-22 inches (male);
18-21 inches (female)**

WEIGHT:
30-55 pounds

LIFE EXPECTANCY:
12-15 years

GROUP:
Herding Group

DID YOU KNOW?

- Border Collies can run for more than 50 miles a day.

- A Hungarian Border Collie named Striker opened a non-electric car window with his paw and nose in a world record 11.34 seconds.

- The popular 1995 film *Babe* featured a Border Collie.

- Border Collies are incredibly sensitive to their owner's actions. Many are adept at predicting what an owner may do.

COLOR:
Variety of colors

COAT:
Close-fitting, dense, soft

COLLIE

HISTORY

A sweet and gentle dog, the Collie is an excellent show and family dog. This intelligent and loyal breed is highly trainable and makes for a reliable watchdog. The Collie has two varieties: rough, or full coat, and smooth, or small coat. This is an unsurprisingly energetic breed that is friendly around other animals.

With its Scottish roots, the Collie was widely recognized in the 19th century. Queen Victoria's affinity for the breed helped promote the breed throughout the European continent as well as the United States. In the 20th century, Albert Payson Terhune popularized the Collie with the books *Sunnybank Collies*. The 1943 film *Lassie Come Home* further publicized the Collie.

Left alone for hours or long stretches, the Collie can become reckless and bored and exercise a preference for barking. The breed also makes for a devoted therapy dog. Prospective owners should know that the Collie is a sensitive breed that is acutely aware of antagonizing tones of voice; Collies may become withdrawn if yelled at repeatedly.

CHARACTERISTICS

HEIGHT:
**24-26 inches (male);
22-24 inches (female)**

WEIGHT:
**65-90 pounds (male);
50-70 pounds (female)**

LIFE EXPECTANCY:
7-10 years

GROUP:
Herding Group

DID YOU KNOW?

- President Benjamin Harrison owned a Collie named Dash.

- The 1950s television show *Lassie* immortalized the Collie in popular culture.

- The first Collie was imported to the United States in 1879.

- The Collie has previously been known as Collis, Colley, Coally, and Coaly.

**COLOR:
Sable, black**

**COAT:
Straight, harsh**

GERMAN SHEPHERD

HISTORY

The imposing and versatile German Shepherd Dog is a fearless and inspiring dog. The breed is extremely protective of his family and home and incredibly trainable. The German Shepherd is a valuable asset for law enforcement and agencies, and it's also a common service dog, too.

German cavalry captain Max von Stephanitz developed the breed in the second half of the 19th century. The captain sought a dog that could be used for police and military work, and by 1899, the breed was registered in Germany. In World War I, the German Shepherd's name was changed in the United Kingdom to Alsatian. Breeders in the United States later changed the German Shepherd's name to Shepherd Dog. The American Kennel Club registered a German Shepherd in 1912.

For prospective owners unwilling to commit to a demanding breed, the German Shepherd is likely not an ideal dog. This breed needs mental and physical stimulation, a job, and, no doubt, a healthy dose of daily exercise. However, despite the German Shepherd's size, he can easily adjust to apartment or condo living so long as he has plenty of outdoors stimulation.

CHARACTERISTICS

HEIGHT:
24-26 inches (male);
22-24 inches (female)

WEIGHT:
65-90 pounds (male);
50-70 pounds (female)

LIFE EXPECTANCY:
7-10 years

GROUP:
Herding Group

DID YOU KNOW?

- One famous German Shepherd, Rin Tin Tin, became a Hollywood star and appeared in more than two dozen films following his rescue from a World War I battlefield.

- Buddy, the first Seeing Eye Dog, was a German Shepherd who lived in the 1920s.

- True to his herding roots, the German Shepherd has a strong tendency to remain constantly within his owner's field of vision.

- The breed's original German name is Deutscher Schäferhund.

COLOR:
Sable, black

COAT:
Straight, harsh

PEMBROKE WELSH CORGI

HISTORY

Confident, athletic, and strong, the Pembroke Welsh Corgi packs a lot of bite in a small package. This extremely popular herding breed is an affectionate companion that makes for a stellar family pet (just ask longtime Corgi owner Queen Elizabeth II). Like the Cardigan Welsh Corgi, the Pembroke Welsh Corgi was developed in Wales; however, the Pembroke is smaller and lacks a tail.

The Pembroke's ancestry can be traced back more than 900 years. Flemish farmers imported the breed into western Wales. Breeders crossed the Pembroke and Cardigan in the 19th century. The Pembroke was ultimately recognized as its own breed in 1934.

The Pembroke Welsh Corgi is a superb watchdog and a loyal family member. True to his herding instincts, training is necessary to curtail the breed's ankle nipping tendencies. Owners should also make sure to watch their Corgi's diet, for this breed can rapidly gain weight and open itself to a host of health problems. And, while loyal, the Pembroke is also rambunctious; training and rule setting are critical at a young age.

CHARACTERISTICS

HEIGHT:
10-12 inches

WEIGHT:
**Up to 30 pounds (male);
Up to 28 pounds (female)**

LIFE EXPECTANCY:
12-13 years

GROUP:
Herding Group

DID YOU KNOW?

- After she received first Pembroke, Susan, in 1933, Queen Elizabeth II owned at least one Pembroke until 2018.

- The words "cor" and "gi" together mean "dwarf dog" in Welsh.

- The Pembroke is one of the Herding Group's smallest members.

- The breed is known for its foxlike face.

COLOR:
Fawn, sable, red, black, tan

COAT:
Short, thick, weather-resistant

SHETLAND SHEEPDOG

HISTORY

The quick and obedient Shetland Sheepdog is one of the most intelligent dog breeds, according to experts. Excellent around his family, the Shetland is nevertheless suspicious of strangers. The breed also loves to bark and yap, a problematic trait for professionals gone from their homes all day. Many Shetlands will spin and jump in circles when excited—a quirky trait known as the "Sheltie spin."

The Shetland hails from the Shetland Islands, located about 50 miles north of Scotland south of the Arctic Circle. The breed was brought to England and Scotland in the early 1800s. By the end of the century, however, excessive crossbreeding led breeders to refine the Shetland. The American Kennel Club registered its first Shetland, Lord Scott, in 1911.

CHARACTERISTICS

HEIGHT:
13-16 inches

WEIGHT:
15-25 pounds

LIFE EXPECTANCY:
12-14 years

GROUP:
Herding Group

Shetlands do fine alongside other household pets, including cats. They learn well when lauded for good behavior, and treats are always a welcome reward. Grooming sessions are compulsory to maintain the breed's rich coat. The Shetland also enjoys chasing people, animals, and objects—including cars and airplanes.

DID YOU KNOW?

- English Collie breeders protested against the breed's original name, Shetland Collie. Their protests ultimately led to the change of name.

- The Shetland, however, has also gone by the names Lilliputian Collie, Toonie Dog, and Fairy Dog.

- The Shetland historically excels at obedience competitions.

- Today, the Shetland is rare in its native Shetland Islands.

COLOR:
Blue merle, sable

COAT:
Long, straight, harsh

AIREDALE TERRIER

HISTORY

The versatile Airedale Terrier is a robust and mischievous breed that has been used for retrieving, hunting, and competing. Known as stubborn yet smart, the Airedale is independent and energetic. This dog loves to bark, chase, dig, and play, so owners uninterested in providing the breed with plenty of activity should steer clear of this breed.

Experts believe the Airedale was developed sometime in the middle of the 19th century. The breed's roots can be found in the Aire Valley in northern England. This Industrial Revolution-era breed hunted small animals like foxes, rats, and badgers. The breed's swimming abilities improved, and in World War I, the Airedale Terrier assisted the British Army and the Red Cross on the battlefield as a guard and messenger dog.

Thanks to the breed's loyal and brave personality, the Airedale makes for an excellent watchdog. This is a fine family dog that gets along quite well with children. But while they are often aloof and comical, Airedales can be aggressive with other dogs. The breed is also a poor choice for owners with cats.

96

CHARACTERISTICS

HEIGHT:
23 inches

WEIGHT:
50-70 pounds

LIFE EXPECTANCY:
11-14 years

GROUP:
Terrier Group

DID YOU KNOW?

- The Airedale is the largest of all terriers.

- Famous American author John Steinbeck owned Airedales.

- Numerous presidents, including Woodrow Wilson and Calvin Coolidge, also owned Airedales.

- The American Kennel Club recognized the Airedale in 1888.

COLOR:
Black, gold

COAT:
Hard, dense, wiry

BORDER TERRIER

HISTORY

The approachable and friendly Border Terrier is a trainable dog that's excellent around children and independent in spirit. Yet the Border Terrier is capable of a host of mischievous antics, and owners should know that the breed requires plentiful exercise and stimulation. The Border Terrier is also a popular therapy dog that is adept at comforting the sick, young, and elderly.

The Border Terrier has existed for at least 300 years. It originated in the northeastern England near Scotland where it helped hunt foxes. The Border Terrier's popularity grew in the early 20th century, and the American Kennel Club recognized the breed in 1930.

A bored Border Terrier is a destructive Border Terrier. Runs, walks, games—ideally multiple times a day—are sound ideas. The breed has a serious prey drive that, coupled with a penchant for chasing, can lead to perilous situations, specifically involving vehicles. A sturdy fence and a strong leash are a necessity with this dog. Owners should remember that this is a people-oriented breed that should be socialized extremely well as a puppy.

CHARACTERISTICS

HEIGHT:
12-15 inches

WEIGHT:
13-15.5 pounds (male);
11.5-14 pounds (female)

LIFE EXPECTANCY:
12-15 years

GROUP:
Terrier Group

DID YOU KNOW?

- In 1930, Netherbyers Ricky became the first registered Border Terrier in the United States.

- The Border Terrier's weather-resistant coat helps repel grime.

- The breed's thick skin helps protect it from bites and cuts.

- An 18th century Arthur Wentworth painting depicts two Border Terriers.

COLOR:
Red,
grizzle and tan,
blue and tan,
wheaten

COAT:
Short, dense, wiry

BULL TERRIER

HISTORY

A good-natured and playful dog, the Bull Terrier is a people-oriented breed with a mischievous temperament. With its triangle-shaped eyes, this muscular dog is full of energy and has a loving personality. Its distinct oval-shaped head has appeared in scores of films, from *Toy Story* to *The Mask*.

The Bull Terrier's complex history dates back to the first half of the 19th century. The breed's ancestors likely include the Bulldog and the extinct English White Terrier. At some point, these ancestors were crossed with the Spanish Pointers. The breed was refined in the second half of the century by way of an Englishman named James Hinks.

The Bull Terrier enjoys outdoor games, be it fetch or other toy-oriented pastimes. The breed also typically only barks for good reason and requires socialization at an early age. Prospective owners should know that the dog's coat requires little grooming.

CHARACTERISTICS

HEIGHT:
21-22 inches

WEIGHT:
50-70 pounds

LIFE EXPECTANCY:
12-13 years

GROUP:
Terrier Group

DID YOU KNOW?

- The Bull Terrier has been featured in a host of famous advertising campaigns for beer and department stores.

- The breed was once nick-named "White Cavalier" after it became fashionable among wealthy gentlemen.

- The first Bull Terrier registered with the American Kennel Club in 1885 was named Nellie II.

- The breed is often referred to as a "kid in a dog suit" thanks to its playful temperament.

COLOR:
Variety of colors

COAT:
Short, flat, harsh

CAIRN TERRIER

HISTORY

Originally bred for hunting vermin, the Cairn Terrier is a small yet energetic breed that has a penchant to chase and root out small animals. This breed enjoys walks, games, playtime with children, and companionship. This rugged and relatively low-maintenance dog requires minimal grooming.

The Cairn Terrier's origins can be found in the Western Isles of Scotland. Alongside other terrier breeds, the Cairn roamed Scottish game preserves for centuries. By the end of the 19th century, breeders refined the Cairn, and the American Kennel Club recognized the breed in 1913.

Thanks to its small size, the breed is suitable for apartment life and can readily adapt to different kinds of homes. And because of the Cairn's intelligence, training should feature lively, challenging activities. The breed is smart enough to learn a host of tricks and commands.

CHARACTERISTICS

HEIGHT:
10 inches (male);
9.5 inches (female)

WEIGHT:
14 pounds (male);
13 pounds (female)

LIFE EXPECTANCY:
13-15 years

GROUP:
Terrier Group

DID YOU KNOW?

- Toto, arguably the most famous Cairn Terrier of all time, was a star in the famous film *The Wizard of Oz.*

- The breed was formerly known as the "Short-haired Skye Terrier."

- Experts believe the "Short-haired Skye Terrier" strain was founded by Captain Martin Macleod of Drynoch, Isle of Skye.

- The Cairn Terrier's coat usually darkens with age.

COLOR:
Variety of colors

COAT:
Hard, weather-resistant

MINIATURE SCHNAUZER

HISTORY

Developed in Germany from the Standard Schnauzer in the second half of the 19th century, the Miniature Schnauzer is a fine family dog with a cheerful and friendly disposition. The breed's lineage dates back to at least the 1400s. While the breed was first exhibited in 1899, the Miniature Schnauzer's popularity grew following World War II. Today, the breed is bred worldwide, and with its loyalty, energy, and fun-loving nature, it's easy to understand the Miniature Schnauzer's appeal.

The Standard Schnauzer was crossbred with smaller breeds like the Miniature Pinscher, Affenpinscher, and most likely the Poodle. A black female Miniature Schnauzer named Findel born in October 1888 is the earliest recorded member of the breed.

This is an eager-to-please, obedient dog. However, many Miniature Schnauzers display a stubbornness that can be frustrating for owners. Luckily, this breed is very easy to train, and intervention at an early age can help curtail poor behaviors. He's also a low-shedding dog that easily makes for an affectionate and loving family member.

CHARACTERISTICS

HEIGHT:
12-14 inches

WEIGHT:
11-20 pounds

LIFE EXPECTANCY:
12-15 years

GROUP:
Terrier Group

DID YOU KNOW?

- The Miniature Schnauzer is the most popular of the three Schnauzer breeds, according to American Kennel Club registrations.

- Unlike other terriers, the Miniature Schnauzer does not have British ancestors.

- While the American Kennel Club classifies the Miniature Schnauzer as a terrier, the Club classifies the Standard Schnauzer as a member of the Working group.

- A host of celebrities and politicians, such as Bob Dole and Mary Tyler Moore, have owned Miniature Schnauzers.

COLOR:
Salt and pepper, black and silver, solid black

COAT:
Hard, wiry

RAT TERRIER

HISTORY

A proud all-American original, the Rat Terrier is a renowned rat catcher that exhibits the usual terrier traits. This farm dog and hunter, which comes in two sizes, is masterful at catching pesky rodents, yet he also makes for a lovable family member.

The Rat Terrier's ancestors include the Bull Terrier, Manchester Terrier, Whippet, and Italian Greyhound, among other breeds. By the 1940s, the Rat Terrier's popularity waned, and the breed's numbers didn't recover until the 1970s.

The Rat Terrier is incredibly easy to groom. Rat Terriers are also very perceptive and attune to their owner's needs. Though certainly small enough for apartments, the breed's high energy levels can result in daylong barking.

CHARACTERISTICS

HEIGHT:
**10-13 inches (miniature);
13-18 inches (standard)**

WEIGHT:
10-25 pounds

LIFE EXPECTANCY:
12-18 years

GROUP:
Terrier Group

DID YOU KNOW?

- A Rat Terrier appeared in the 1935 Shirley Temple movie *The Little Colonel*.

- One Rat Terrier is reported to have caught more than 2,500 rats in about seven hours.

- President Theodore Roosevelt was an especially enthusiastic fan of Rat Terriers.

- The breed's ears can be dropped or erect.

COLOR:
Variety of colors

COAT:
Short, smooth, shiny

SCOTTISH TERRIER

HISTORY

The independent and confident Scottish Terrier is an affectionate and vocal breed that enjoys hunting backyard rodents and a daily walk. Opinionated, serious, and maybe even a bit stubborn, the Scottish Terrier is nevertheless a breed devoted to his human family. He's naturally suspicious of strangers and isn't too interested about other dogs, either.

Originally bred to be a hunter of foxes and badgers, the Scottish Terrier is most likely one of Scotland's oldest breeds. Its history is somewhat obscure, but it is known that the Romans, following their invasion of Great Britain, admired the breed. Hundreds of years later, James I of England, a Scot by birth, gifted Scottish Terriers to other countries. The breed wasn't brought to the United States until the 1880s.

While certainly trainable, the Scottish Terrier is not the easiest dog to train. He's also not the greatest choice for a family with young children. He likes to dig, too. And his coat requires thorough brushing several times a week. Despite those perceived negatives, the Scottish Terrier is, for the right owner that enjoys a terrier's temperament, a fantastic addition to the family.

CHARACTERISTICS

HEIGHT:
10-11 inches

WEIGHT:
19-22 pounds (male);
18-21 pounds (female)

LIFE EXPECTANCY:
9-15 years

GROUP:
Terrier Group

DID YOU KNOW?

- Dake, the first registered Scottish Terrier in the United States, was born in 1884.

- President Franklin Roosevelt owned a Scottish Terrier named Fala. Presidents Dwight D. Eisenhower and George W. Bush also owned Scottish Terriers during their time in the White House.

- Hollywood legends like Humphrey Bogart and Bette Davis each owned a Scottish Terrier.

- Thanks to the breed's persistent personality, the Scottish Terrier is also known by the nickname "the Diehard."

COLOR:
Black, wheaten

COAT:
Broken, hard, wiry

WEST HIGHLAND WHITE TERRIER

HISTORY

A busy and energetic little dog, the West Highland White Terrier is a people-oriented breed that is beloved for his thick white coat. Cheerful and certainly adorable, the "Westie" requires a lot of companionship; this dog can be downright destructive and yappy if bored or alone. And don't expect him to be a cuddly lap dog: the Westie is a busy breed that needs plentiful stimulation.

True to his small-game hunting roots, the Westie, akin to his short-legged relatives, was developed in Scotland in the 19th century from Cairn Terriers. Originally bred to be a rodent exterminator, the Westie was first shown at Scottish dog shows at the very end of the century. The breed began to make appearances at American Kennel Club shows in 1906.

CHARACTERISTICS

HEIGHT:
**11 inches (male);
10 inches (female)**

WEIGHT:
15-20 pounds

LIFE EXPECTANCY:
13-15 years

GROUP:
Terrier Group

Many know the Westie as a cocky breed that is far from shy. Early training and socialization are a must to help mitigate the breed's more destructive and obnoxious behaviors. The Westie's tireless temperament and smarts also make it a solid candidate for dog sports.

DID YOU KNOW?

- The Westie was once known as the Roseneath Terrier and as the Poltalloch Terrier.

- Scotland's Colonel Edward Donald Malcolm is credited with breeding the Westie white after one of his reddish brown Cairn Terriers was shot. It was shot after it was mistaken for a fox.

- A number of brands, including Black & White Scotch Whisky and Juicy Couture, have utilized the Westie's image in advertising campaigns.

- The breed's name was officially changed from Roseneath Terrier to West Highland White Terrier in May 1909.

COLOR:
White

COAT:
Hard, straight, thick

CAVALIER KING CHARLES SPANIEL

HISTORY

An exceptional family pet, the Cavalier King Charles Spaniel is a happy and trustworthy lap dog. One of the largest in its group, the breed's famous soft eyes contribute to it heart-melting expression. The breed also has a strong prey drive that can mean trouble and even danger around moving vehicles.

The toy spaniel was for centuries a favorite of European nobles. Mary, Queen of Scots and King Charles I were especially fond of these dogs. But their popularity declined over time, and eventually these dogs were cross-bred with other breeds like Pugs. By the 19th century, breeders began to refine these spaniels. The American Kennel Club fully recognized the breed in 1995.

Besides chasing objects, the Cavalier King Charles Spaniel enjoys licking and meeting new people. It is also an adaptive breed. Suitable for either large homes or small city apartments, this breed can also easily adapt

CHARACTERISTICS

HEIGHT:
12-13 inches

WEIGHT:
13-18 pounds

LIFE EXPECTANCY:
12-15 years

GROUP:
Toy Group

to an owner's active or couch potato lifestyle. Additionally, the Cavalier King Charles Spaniel is easy to train, and despite its often stubborn personality, this is no dumb dog.

DID YOU KNOW?

- King Charles I of Britain was a fan of the breed.

- The Cavalier King Charles Spaniel appeared on the hit television show *Sex and the City*.

- An American named Roswell Eldridge is credited with helping to revive the breed after generations of crossbreeding.

- The Cavalier King Charles Spaniel is a relative of the English Toy Spaniel.

COLOR:
Blenheim, tricolor, ruby, black and tan

COAT:
Silky

CHIHUAHUA

HISTORY

The smallest dog breed in the world, the Chihuahua is a tiny dog with a big personality. He's alert, curious, and affectionate. This purse puppy is a fiesty and loyal companion that is equally expressive and, obviously, fashionable.

It's unclear how the Chihuahua arrived in Mexico, but these small dogs were discovered in the 1850s. Experts believe the breed is descended from the Toltec people, a Mesoamerican population that inhabited eastern Mexico more than 1,000 years ago. Americans became interested in the dogs in the middle of the 19th century, however, and the breed's popularity grew throughout the 20th century. Stars like Lupe Velez and Xavier Cugat brought the Chihuahua into the mainstream.

Despite its small size, the Chihuahua is not the best breed for small children. He's fragile, likely to nip, and can appear ferocious when provoked. Quality training and socialization are a must at an early age. Chihuahuas usually become very close with their owners, and they may treat strangers with deep suspicion.

CHARACTERISTICS

HEIGHT:
5-8 inches

WEIGHT:
Up to 6 pounds

LIFE EXPECTANCY:
14-16 years

GROUP:
Toy Group

DID YOU KNOW?

- Today, the Chihuahua is a cultural icon. From the Taco Bell mascot to its appearances in movies like *Legally Blonde* and *Beverly Hills Chihuahua*, this small dog is ubiquitous.

- The first American Kennel Club-registered Chihuahua was named Beppie; the registration was in 1908.

- The breed has a long or smooth coat.

- Chihuahuas acquired their name from the Mexican State of Chihuahua.

COLOR:
Any color

COAT:
Soft, close, glossy

HAVANESE

HISTORY

Cuba's sole native breed, the Havanese is an energetic and intelligent small dog that lives for attention. This silky dog is excellent around children, displays goofy behavior, and enjoys sitting on laps. The Havanese is prone to separation anxiety, however, and can become quite anxious if left alone for long stretches of time.

Experts believe the Havanese, which is a relative of the Bichon Frise, was brought to Cuba by Italian or Spanish traders. The breed's ancestors interbred in Cuba, and the dogs that emerged are similar to the breed today. Wealthy Cuban families of the 19th century became enamored with the breed, and European travelers brought these dogs back to the European continent throughout the 1800s. But by the middle of the 20th century, the breed was nearly extinct. Luckily, in the 1970s, the Havanese's numbers rebounded thanks primarily to an American couple.

This rambunctious breed is, in a word, fun. The Havanese is also an excellent therapy dog, due to its easygoing personality. Training should begin at an early age, as this breed can easily develop destructive and obnoxious behavior otherwise.

CHARACTERISTICS

HEIGHT:
8.5-11.5 inches

WEIGHT:
7-13 pounds

LIFE EXPECTANCY:
14-16 years

GROUP:
Toy Group

DID YOU KNOW?

- The American Kennel Club recognized the Havanese in 1995.

- The Havanese is also known as the Habanero.

- Most Havanese dogs today can trace their ancestry to 11 dogs.

- The Havanese's coat developed to protect it from the sun and overheating.

COLOR:
Any color

COAT:
Silky, soft

MALTESE

HISTORY

Lively and charming, the Maltese is a loving companion that enjoys cuddling and, unsurprisingly, attention. This is a people-oriented breed that prioritizes play and, again, attention. Despite his small size, the Maltese still needs daily exercise, and training at a young age is a must.

The Maltese's history dates back more than 2,000 years. The breed charmed Romans and Greeks and was popular among traders. The Greeks even designed tombs for their Maltese friends. Chinese breeders kept the Maltese from extinction in Europe during the Dark Ages. The breed's presence didn't grace the United States until the second half of the 19th century.

The Maltese is incredibly trainable, and, like the Havanese, this breed makes for a fine therapy dog. However, because of the breed's small size, this Maltese may not be a good fit for small children. Prospective owners should know that near-constant grooming is essential to maintain the Maltese's silky coat.

CHARACTERISTICS

HEIGHT:
7-9 inches

WEIGHT:
Up to 7 pounds

LIFE EXPECTANCY:
12-15 years

GROUP:
Toy Group

DID YOU KNOW?

- The Maltese was once known as the "Melitaie Dog."

- The breed was first exhibited in the United States in 1877 and described as the "Maltese Lion Dog"

- The American Kennel Club registered its first Maltese in 1888.

- The breed was once known as "Ye Ancient Dogge of Malta."

COLOR:
White

COAT:
Flat, silky

PAPILLON

HISTORY

The quick and upbeat Papillon is a lot of dog in a small package. Highly intelligent and agile, this little breed is an expressive companion with good looks. Despite his size, the Papillon requires a good deal of daily exercise, and he excels at dog sports and obedience activities.

The Papillon has a storied history among Europe's nobles. Marie Antoinette and Madame de Pompadour were enthusiasts, and the breed can be found in famous paintings by the likes of Goya and Rembrandt. The modern version of the breed—with features like erect ears and predominately white coats—began to appear by the end of the 19th century. In 1915, the American Kennel Club registered its first Papillon.

To combat nervousness, early socialization is a must with this breed; exposures to different people, dogs, sights, and sounds are a necessity. Unlike other toy breeds, the Papillon is less of a lap dog and more of a busy bee. However, similar to other breeds in their group, the Papillon can suffer from serious separation anxiety. This dog needs plenty of attention from their human family.

CHARACTERISTICS

HEIGHT:
8-11 inches

WEIGHT:
5-10 pounds

LIFE EXPECTANCY:
14-16 years

GROUP:
Toy Group

DID YOU KNOW?

- The Papillon's popularity began in the Renaissance era.

- Kirby, a Papillon who won Best in Show at both Westminster and at the World Dog Show in 1999, is one of the best known Papillons.

- The breed's name means "butterfly" in French.

- The Papillon has been previously known as the Belgian Toy Spaniel, Dwarf Continental Spaniel, and Little Squirrel Dog.

COLOR:
White, black and white

COAT:
Short, thick

POMERANIAN

HISTORY

Brave, bold, and personable, the Pomeranian is a descendant of the large sled dog breeds that dominated the world's northernmost countries. The original Pomeranian weighed about eight times as much as today's strains. Today's Pomeranian is nevertheless athletic, smart, and active.

The Pomeranian's popularity is largely a result of Queen Victoria, who fell in love with the breed during an 1888 Italian vacation. Breeders standardized the breed in the early 20th century, and the Pomeranian quickly spread to the United States by the 1920s. By the middle of the 20th century, the Pomeranian was one of the most popular breeds in the United States.

This is an extremely extroverted dog. The Pomeranian does well around both people and other animals, and this curious dog has little fear of larger canines. Owners should train their Pomeranian early to curtail pesky barking habits. This breed can do well in either a small city apartment or a large country home. And like other toy breeds, Pomeranians may not be the best for young children due to their delicate size.

CHARACTERISTICS

HEIGHT:
6-7 inches

WEIGHT:
3-7 pounds

LIFE EXPECTANCY:
12-16 years

GROUP:
Toy Group

DID YOU KNOW?

- The American Kennel Club recognized the Pomeranian in 1900.

- One of Queen Victoria's favorite Pomeranians comforted the queen on her deathbed.

- The breed is a member of a family of breeds known as the "Spitz Group."

- Besides Queen Victoria, other historical figures like Wolfgang Amadeus Mozart and Emile Zola owned Pomeranians.

COLOR:
Any solid color

COAT:
Dense, harsh

PUG

HISTORY

Playful, mischievous, and sometimes stubborn, the Pug is one of the world's oldest breeds. This heartful companion dog is a people-pleaser and somewhat sedentary. The Pug enjoys fun and being funny, and the breed's easygoing temperament makes it an excellent fit for families and children.

Little is known about the Pug's history, but experts believe the breed originated in China. Genetics suggest the Pug is closely related to the Brussels Griffon. The breed was likely brought to Holland in the 1500s, and the Pug eventually became popular among nobles. The American Kennel Club began to register the breed in 1885.

The Pug is likely best known as a playful and even comical dog. He certainly won't mind wearing a costume on Halloween, and he'll no doubt provide owners with a host of silly behavior. In return, he will demand attention and devotion which, luckily, is easy to give.

CHARACTERISTICS

HEIGHT:
10-13 inches

WEIGHT:
14-18 pounds

LIFE EXPECTANCY:
13-15 years

GROUP:
Toy Group

COLOR:
Fawn, black

COAT:
Fine, smooth, glossy

DID YOU KNOW?

- The Pug has charmed famous figures like King Louis XIV, the Duke and Duchess of Windsor, and Empress Josephine.

- Thanks to its flat face, the Pug snorts and snores.

- The Pug's name most likely derives from its facial expression. The expression is similar to marmoset monkeys.

- The breed became the official dog of the Netherlands's House of Orange after a Pug saved the crown prince.

SHIH TZU

HISTORY

The playful and sweet Shih Tzu is first and foremost a companion that desires attention. The breed is one of the world's most popular toy breeds, and it's particularly beloved in the United States and the United Kingdom. The Shih Tzu is an intelligent dog with a sweet disposition.

The breed likely originated in Tibet, as experts believe the Shih Tzu was bred by Tibetan lamas as a small replica of a lion. It was also the house pet for the majority of the Ming Dynasty. The Shih Tzu ultimately lived a pampered life among royals for generations, and throughout the first half of the 20th century, the breed was exported to Europe, Australia, and the United States. The American Kennel Club recognized the Shih Tzu in 1969.

Since he's not demanding or high-strung, the Shih Tzu is a fine canine friend for many, especially the elderly. The Shih Tzu is able to easily entertain himself for hours, so long as he receives some attention throughout the day. The breed is also friendly around, dogs, cats, and children.

126

CHARACTERISTICS

HEIGHT:
9-10.5 inches

WEIGHT:
9-16 pounds

LIFE EXPECTANCY:
10-18 years

GROUP:
Toy Group

DID YOU KNOW?

- The breed's name is pronounced SHEED-zoo.

- In Chinese, the Shih Tzu means "little lion."

- The Chinese called the breed the Chrysanthemum Dog because of the way the Shih Tzu's facial hair grows outward like a flower's petals.

- The breed commonly ranks as one of the most popular dog breeds in the world.

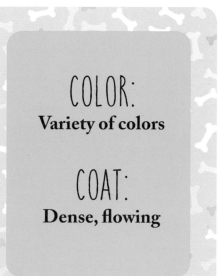

COLOR:
Variety of colors

COAT:
Dense, flowing

YORKSHIRE TERRIER

HISTORY

A compact and feisty breed, the Yorkshire Terrier (or Yorkie) is a curious and humorous dog that appeals to the masses. The tiny breed has been both a member of high society and the working class. While small enough to fit in a purse, the Yorkshire Terrier is likely not a breed for small children because of its size and yappy personality.

The Yorkie's roots can be traced back to the northern English counties of Yorkshire and Lancashire. The breed first appeared in northern England in the mid-1800s after Scottish weavers brought their Scottish terriers with them when they migrated to England (those terriers are part of the Yorkie's genetic mix). The Yorkie was nimble enough to pursue rodents in textile mills, and he could also be found serving similar duties in coal mines. By the late-1800s, the breed gained popularity among wealthy English women.

Today, Yorkies are known for their silky, floor-length hypoallergenic coat and yappy personality. They do better around older children than younger children. Expect years of companionship with this small breed.

128

CHARACTERISTICS

HEIGHT:
7-8 inches

WEIGHT:
7 pounds

LIFE EXPECTANCY:
11-15 years

GROUP:
Toy Group

DID YOU KNOW?

- Because of their digestive systems, Yorkshire Terriers can be picky eaters.

- Is your home too chilly or too humid? If so, do what you can to remediate the problem. Yorkshire Terriers dislike drastic temperature changes. They're indoor dogs, after all.

- A Yorkshire Terrier named Smoky fought alongside American soldiers in the Pacific Theater during World War II. She even helped complete construction of an airfield by pulling a telephone line through a 70-foot pipe.

- One of the smallest dogs ever recorded was a Yorkshire Terrier named Sylvia. The tiny terrier was 2.5 inches tall, 3.5 inches long, and weighed 4 ounces.

COLOR:
Black, brown, gray, white

COAT:
Flat, water-resistant, coarse

BICHON FRISE

HISTORY

A small, cheerful, and fluffy dog, the Bichon Frise is a sweet and affectionate breed that craves attention and a good cuddle. The breed belongs to the same family of dogs as the Havanese, Maltese, and Bolognese. The Bichon Frise is an altogether cheerful and intelligent breed that, because of its size, may not be a good fit for small children.

For centuries, the Bichon Frise was a favorite among European nobility. But following the French Revolution, the breed's popularity plumpeted. The down-and-out Bichon caught the attention of street performers and, soon enough, the Bichon was a common sight in circus acts. World War I and II hampered the breed's numbers, but by the middle of the century, the Bichon's popularity rebounded. The breed arrived in the United States in the 1950s.

Thanks to his intelligence, the Bichon is incredibly trainable. Training should begin at an early age, and prospective owners should know that this breed can be difficult to house train. The Bichon also loathes being left alone for long stretches of time.

130

CHARACTERISTICS

HEIGHT:
9.5-11.5 inches

WEIGHT:
12-18 pounds

LIFE EXPECTANCY:
14-15 years

GROUP:
Non-Sporting Group

DID YOU KNOW?

- The breed's name is pronounced BEE-shawn FREEzy.

- In French, the Bichon's name means "curly coated."

- The Bichon is known for its "Bichon Blitz," a random spurt of energy involving running and barking. It typically lasts for about one minute before the dog settles down.

- The American Kennel Club recognized the Bichon in 1973.

COLOR:
White

COAT:
Soft, dense (undercoat); coarse, curly (outercoat)

BOSTON TERRIER

HISTORY

An all-American original, the Boston Terrier is a gentle and loving companion. The Boston Terrier is incredibly loyal to his human family, and he's adaptable to his environment, be it a large house or a small apartment. The Boston Terrier is a sturdy, impressive dog that also does well around children and other pets.

The story behind the Boston Terrier's development is unclear, but what is known is that a dog named Judge played a major role. Judge, a cross between a Bulldog and the extinct English White Terrier, was bred with a white dog named Burnett's Gyp, and this breeding produced a puppy named Well's Eph. Further breeding developed the Boston Terrier into a smaller and more attractive dog. The American Kennel Club recognized the breed in 1893.

This personable breed loves people. From greeting strangers to snuggling with his owner, this dog is a social canine. Many Boston Terriers have a good sense of humor, too.

CHARACTERISTICS

HEIGHT:
15-17 inches

WEIGHT:
12-25 pounds

LIFE EXPECTANCY:
11-13 years

GROUP:
Non-Sporting Group

DID YOU KNOW?

- The Boston Terrier has been Boston University's official mascot since 1922.

- In 1979, the Massachusetts state legislature named the Boston Terrier the state's official dog.

- The Boston Terrier's nickname is the "American Gentleman" due, in part, to his manners.

- Boston Terriers have been known as Round Heads, Bullet Heads, and Bull Terriers.

COLOR:
Brindle

COAT:
Smooth, bright, fine

133

BULLDOG

HISTORY

The tenacious and courageous Bulldog is an incredibly friendly and adaptable breed. Famous for his wrinkled face, upturned nose, and muscular build, the Bulldog is also celebrated as England's unofficial mascot. This good-natured breed embodies determination and grit.

While today he's known as a gentle family dog, the Bulldog's ancestors were once ferocious canines that fought in bloodsports. In a vicious activity known as bull-baiting, spectators watched as the breed fought a pack of dogs. These violent games were outlawed in England by the 19th century, a move that severely curtailed the Bulldog's numbers. Luckily, breeders responded by moderating the Bulldog's aggressive persona. Today's Bulldog made its way to the United States by the 1880s. In World War II, surprisingly similar physical characteristics between the breed and Prime Minister Winston Churchill catapulted the Bulldog's popularity to new heights.

The Bulldog is excellent around children, and he's a great fit for many families. He can adapt to large

CHARACTERISTICS

HEIGHT:
14-15 inches

WEIGHT:
**50 pounds (male);
40 pounds (female)**

LIFE EXPECTANCY:
8-10 years

GROUP:
Non-Sporting Group

homes or small apartments. Prospective owners should know that this breed must live indoors, for it's unable to withstand excessive heat and humidity. Bulldogs also cannot swim, since the breed's frame inhibits it from being able to tread water.

DID YOU KNOW?

- The Bulldog is the United States Marine Corps's official mascot.

- President Calvin Coolidge owned a Bulldog named "Boston Beans," and President Warren G. Harding's Bulldog was named "Old Boy."

- Handsome Dan, Yale University's Bulldog mascot, is believed to be the first animal mascot of any sport.

- Since 1956, the same line of Bulldogs has served as mascots for the University of Georgia.

COLOR:
Variety of colors

COAT:
Straight, flat, close, smooth

CHOW CHOW

HISTORY

Aloof, muscular, and serious, the Chow Chow is an ancient breed known for his loyalty and furrowed face. The dog hails from northern China and was bred for hunting and herding. Today, this teddy bear-looking, medium-sized breed is best known as a devoted family member.

Breeds akin to the Chow Chow date back more than 2,000 years. They found homes among Chinese nobles, especially an 8th century emperor who had 5,000 Chow-like dogs in his kennels. The breed first reached the Western parts of the world in the 1700s; the Chow Chow was exhibited in the United States by the end of the 19th century. The American Kennel Club recognized the breed in 1903.

Thanks to his low activity level, the Chow Chow manages well in homes large or small. Early training and socialization are highly recommended to curtail the breed's penchant for dominating behavior. While the Chow Chow is friendly in appearance, parents should know that it can be standoffish around children.

CHARACTERISTICS

HEIGHT:
17-20 inches

WEIGHT:
45-70 pounds

LIFE EXPECTANCY:
8-12 years

GROUP:
Non-Sporting Group

DID YOU KNOW?

- An adult Chow Chow has a blue-black tongue. The dog's tongue darkens during the first weeks of life.

- The breed's name in Chinese translates to "puffy lion dog."

- Because of the Chow Chow's straight rear legs, the breed has a stilted gait.

- Jo-Fi, a Chow Chow assistant of Sigmund Freud, worked with the famous psychoanalyst and helped provide clues to the mental states of Freud's clients.

COLOR:
Cream, gold, red, blue, black

COAT:
Abundant, dense, straight, (rough coat); hard, dense (smooth coat)

DALMATIAN

HISTORY

Active, intelligent, and playful, the Dalmatian is an alert breed that makes for an excellent family pet. This curious dog has a relatively unknown ancestry, but it has served as a hunting dog, watchdog, and war dog in its storied past. It's perhaps most famous for its dark spots; today, it is the only spotted dog in existence.

The Dalmatian, experts believe, traces its roots to the eastern Croatian region of Dalmatia. The breed's popularity in Great Britain soared in the 19th century because of its assignment as a "carriage dog." These carriage dog Dalmatians protected horses from vicious stray dogs. In 1888, the American Kennel Club recognized the breed.

The book *The Hundred and One Dalmatians* and its subsequent film adaptations popularized the Dalmatian throughout the second half of the 20th century. Sadly, many owners did not anticipate the breed's active nature, resulting in many abandoned dogs. Prospective owners should know that the Dalmatian is a people-oriented breed that should be in lockstep with his family's happenings.

CHARACTERISTICS

HEIGHT:
19-24 inches

WEIGHT:
45-70 pounds

LIFE EXPECTANCY:
11-13 years

GROUP:
Non-Sporting Group

DID YOU KNOW?

- Dalmatians are born without spots.

- In both advertisements and popular culture, Dalmatians are often seen working alongside firefighters.

- Dalmatians and horses are natural friends.

- Other names for the Dalmatian include the English Coach Dog, the Spotted Dick, the Plum Pudding Dog, and the Carriage Dog.

COLOR:
White with liver spots

COAT:
Short, dense, glossy

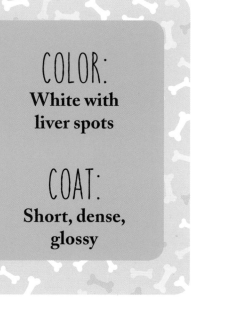

FRENCH BULLDOG

HISTORY

The charming and attentive breed, the French Bulldog or "Frenchie" is a fun dog that makes for an excellent companion. This intelligent breed, famous for its bat ears and half-flat, half-domed skull, is also a reliable watchdog thanks to its alert nature. Today, the small yet compact Frenchie is particularly favored in large cities.

The French Bulldog is a descendent of the British Toy Bulldog. These small dogs grew popular in France among lace makers throughout the 1800s. Eventually, the toy dogs were crossed with terriers and Pugs, and this new breed soon drew interest from members of Parisian high society. The Frenchie's popularity grew in Europe and the United States by the end of the century.

The Frenchie does poorly in hot and humid climates; air conditioning is a must with this breed. He'll also snore, grunt, and snort, thanks to his flat face. But for owners unable to provide an active lifestyle for their dog, the Frenchie might be a great choice: this breed requires little more than 20 minutes of exercise each day.

CHARACTERISTICS

HEIGHT:
11-13 inches

WEIGHT:
Less than 28 pounds

LIFE EXPECTANCY:
10-12 years

GROUP:
Non-Sporting Group

DID YOU KNOW?

- The breed's name in French is Bouledogue français.

- Because of the French Bulldogs's frame and inherent respiratory issues, the breed can easily drown.

- The French Bulldog is a highly sensitive breed and does not respond well to angry criticism.

- Celebrities like Leonardo DiCaprio, Hugh Jackman, Lady Gaga, and Zach Braff have been spotted with French Bulldogs.

COLOR:
White, cream, fawn

COAT:
Short, smooth

POODLE

HISTORY

Fiercely intelligent and highly humorous, the Poodle is an immensely popular breed known for his dashing looks and clipped coat. This extroverted breed is an excellent family dog that loves to entertain. The Poodle also performs well in dog sports and competitions.

Experts believe the Poodle originated in Germany. The Standard Poodle originated more than 400 years ago; it was an excellent water dog and retriever. Hunters shaved parts of the dog's body to help with range of movement in the water and to protect body parts from frigid temperatures. The breed was also popular among nobles and in circuses. Eventually, breeders bred the Poodle down to the Miniature, and the toy breed emerged in the United States in the early 20th century. The American Kennel Club registered its first Poodle in 1886.

The Poodle is incredibly protective of his family and may be slow to warm up to other people. In fact, this breed is best off being a part of nearly every family activity. This dog needs plenty of stimulation.

CHARACTERISTICS

HEIGHT:
**10-15 inches (miniature);
more than 15 inches (standard)**

WEIGHT:
**10-15 pounds (miniature);
40-70 pounds (standard)**

LIFE EXPECTANCY:
10-18 years

GROUP:
Non-Sporting Group

Prospective owners should also know that the Poodle's coat is non-shedding but requires consistent grooming.

DID YOU KNOW?

- The Poodle is known as the Caniche, or "duck dog," in France.

- Poodles became immensely popular in the United States following World War II.

- French nobles, including Louis XIV and Louis XVI, had an affinity for the breed.

- The Poodle's rounded tufts of hair are called pompons.

COLOR:
Variety of colors

COAT:
Dense, curly, woolly

SHIBA INU

HISTORY

The ancient and adaptable Shiba Inu is Japan's most popular companion dog. With its foxlike appearance, the Shiba Inu is a bold, smart breed that needs training and socialization at an early age. Sometimes catlike but always affectionate, the Shiba Inu is a small dog with a lot of bite.

An ancient breed that is believed to have been around since about 300 B.C., the Shiba Inu served for centuries as a hunter in Japan. The breed was nearly extinct by the end of World War II due to distemper, but it luckily recovered. The Shiba Inu arrived in the United States in 1954, and its popularity has grown over the past 60 years.

The Shiba Inu can be stubborn, and it isn't particularly easy to train. However, many owners will find their Shiba Inu to be playful and curious. This loyal breed is naturally suspicious of strangers, and it will likely have a favorite family member. Early exposure to other dogs and pets is paramount; the Shiba Inu doesn't share very well and can act territorial or even aggressive around other animals.

DID YOU KNOW?

- In Japanese, the Shiba Inu's name translates to "brushwood dog."

- Japan declared the Shiba Inu to be a precious natural resource in 1936.

CHARACTERISTICS

HEIGHT:
14.5-16.5 inches (male);
13.5-15.5 inches (female)

LIFE EXPECTANCY:
13-16 years

WEIGHT:
23 pounds (male);
17 pounds (female)

GROUP:
Non-Sporting Group

COLOR:
Black, brown, gray, white

COAT:
Flat, water-resistant, coarse

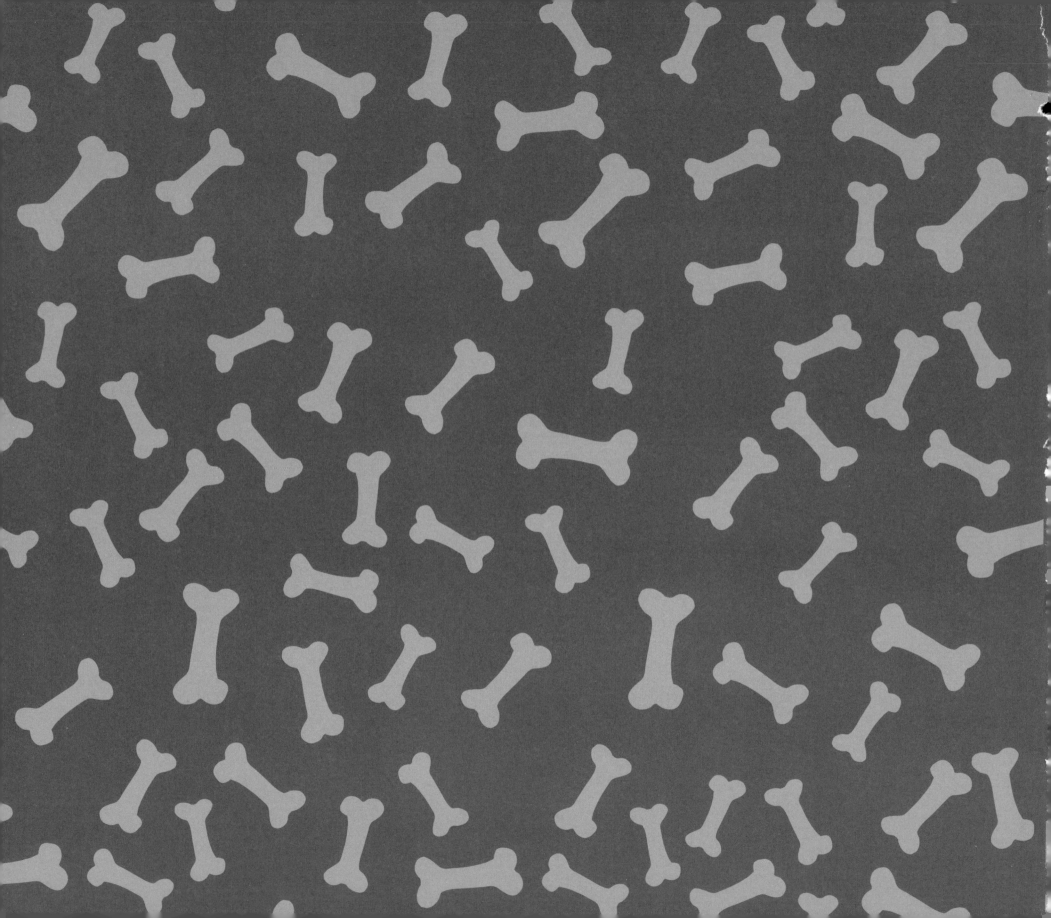